LISA BROMFIELD

The Magic Inside You
How to Create Lasting Joy and Inner Peace Through the Healing Power of Self-Love and Forgiveness

First published by Mother Tree Resources: www.mothertreeresources.com 2025

Copyright © 2025 by Lisa Bromfield

All rights reserved. No part of this publication may be reproduced, stored or transmitted in any form or by any means, electronic, mechanical, photocopying, recording, scanning, or otherwise without written permission from the publisher. It is illegal to copy this book, post it to a website, or distribute it by any other means without permission.

Designations used by companies to distinguish their products are often claimed as trademarks. All brand names and product names used in this book and on its cover are trade names, service marks, trademarks and registered trademarks of their respective owners. The publishers and the book are not associated with any product or vendor mentioned in this book. None of the companies referenced within the book have endorsed the book.

Lisa Bromfield has no responsibility for the persistence or accuracy of URLs for external or third-party Internet Websites referred to in this publication and does not guarantee that any content on such Websites is, or will remain, accurate or appropriate. Quotes in this book are widely attributed and offered in the spirit of inspiration. They may not be exact or verifiable, but reflect the essence of the wisdom shared.

Mental Health Disclaimer

The information presented in this book is for educational and informational purposes only and is not intended as a substitute for professional medical or mental health advice, diagnosis, or treatment. The author is not a licensed mental health professional. Readers are advised to consult a qualified healthcare provider regarding any mental health concerns. If you are experiencing a mental health crisis, please contact a licensed professional, call the National Suicide Prevention Lifeline at 1-800-273-8255, or text HOME to 741741.

First edition

Cover art by Mark Cort

This book was professionally typeset on Reedsy.
Find out more at reedsy.com

Dedication

To my beloved brothers, thank you for being part of my soul's journey. Through the trials and the triumphs, your presence helped shape the light I now stand in.

To my dearest friends, of over twenty years—Laurie and Skip—thank you for believing in me when I couldn't always believe in myself. Your love helped bring this book to life.

I also want to thank my nephew Ian—thank you for understanding me, for believing in me, and for sharing a journey that led us both to new beginnings.

Contents

Acknowledgments	iii
Preface	iv
My Path as an Author and Inspirational Speaker	1
Follow the Yellow Brick Road	4
Follow the Signs	6
What Is a Spiritual Awakening?	9
An Invitation to Grow	11
What Was My Catalyst?	14
Finding a Teacher, Energy Worker, and/or Mentor	17
A Course in Miracles: The Shift from Fear to Love	20
Stepping Into My Calling	25
Follow the Universe's Plan	27
What is Spirit, Our Higher Self, and our Guides?	29
The Journey with TikTok	33
Embracing the Journey	36
Abandonment	38
What Is Self-Love?	40
Inner Child Work	42
The Power of Forgiveness	44
What is Cord Cutting?	47
Karmic Lessons	50
Boundaries and Relationships	53
Letting Go — The Soft Power of Surrender	58
Grief and Loss	61
Energy Work	63
Creating a Daily Practice	69

Plant Medicine	72
Movement as Medicine	74
Nature	76
Grounding and Centering	79
Spiritual Hygiene and Protection	81
Sound Healing	84
Fear	88
Solitude	91
Journaling: Feel It to Heal It	93
What You Resist, Persists	96
The Negativity Bias	99
What Are Beliefs?	101
The Law of Attraction	106
Thoughts and Words Create Your Reality	109
Meditation	112
The Power of Embracing the Present Moment	115
How to Manifest Your Desires	117
Inspired Action	119
Becoming a Death Doula	121
Death As Transformation	128
My Greatest Teachers	131
The Forgiveness Journey with Mom	136
Tony Robbins: Unleash the Power Within	140
The Importance of a Role Model	144
One Size Does Not Fit All	146
The Journey Back to Love	148
Unbecoming: Final Thoughts	150
Afterword	152
Sources and Inspirations	154
Praise for Lisa Bromfield	156

Acknowledgments

I want to acknowledge the incredible souls who helped bring this book into being.

Catherine Dunn, my brilliant developmental editor, was instrumental in restructuring the book. Her insight and clarity allowed the deeper threads of my story to emerge and take shape with purpose.

Aelah Sophia, my intuitive and gifted publisher—also deeply rooted in the healing arts—felt the heart space from which I wrote. She assisted in crafting the book so that it would truly flow for the reader and provided important insights along the way. She encouraged me to stretch further as a writer, to be even more vulnerable and expansive, and I am so grateful for that gentle but powerful nudge.

A heartfelt thank you to Mark Cort for designing the cover of this book, beautifully capturing the essence of our journey down the yellow brick road.

Preface

The magic is already inside you. You may not have tapped into it yet, but it's there—I promise you. I know because I discovered the magic inside me…

This book chronicles the journey of my spiritual awakening and transformation. It shares how I embarked on a path of forgiveness, first with myself, then with my family, breaking free from the emotional shackles that once held me captive. By choosing to confront my deepest traumas and heal the wounds of the past, I was able to create a renewed and empowered version of myself.

What I've come to understand is that healing on the spiritual journey is truly an inside job.

It requires patience, trust, and deep faith. The simple truth is—transformation is often messy and painful. You will be stretched, just as I was, and you'll be asked to sit with discomfort as you grow. At times, the emotional roller coaster may have you questioning your sanity. But I promise you—this is all part of the process.

The rewards, though, are profound. On the other side of the pain, you will uncover your deeper purpose, begin to live more authentically, and start honoring your true essence. And that is where the real magic begins.

I will share the methods I used to create a new belief system—one that allowed me to love myself unconditionally and release all judgment of my past experiences. By fully surrendering to the Universe and letting go of control, I was able to manifest extraordinary and unimaginable things into my life. It is my deepest hope that through this book, you will, too.

My Path as an Author and Inspirational Speaker

"Listen to the stirrings of your soul, follow your heart, for it knows the direction toward your highest calling."
- *Rumi*

In September 2022, I received an unexpected invitation from a Facebook acquaintance to visit The Villages in Central Florida. This retirement community had an interesting reputation as the "Disney World" for adults. However, during my visit, I discovered a tight-knit spiritual community.

When I returned from the trip, I began searching for different Facebook pages associated with The Villages, hoping that perhaps I could create a niche for myself there. I reached out to a woman who was a yoga teacher, introducing myself, sharing a bit about my practice, and planting a seed for potential collaboration.

She replied, "I'm preparing for the 2nd Annual Women's Spiritual Retreat in February, and I just happen to have one spot open for a speaker. Let's connect on Zoom."

Before our call, Maryann reviewed my videos and shared one with her

The Magic Inside You

team. When we spoke on the Zoom call, the connection was immediate and natural. She officially invited me to be one of the retreat's speakers. This opportunity felt monumental.

Until that point, my public speaking experience had been limited to two twenty-minute talks at a metaphysical church. I meticulously prepared my PowerPoint presentation for the weekend Retreat and practiced relentlessly every morning, refining and rehearsing my delivery. I stood in my mobile home living room, imagining the feeling of touching the lives of these women in a special way. I did not want to disappoint them.

The day finally arrived. I stood before an audience of seventy-five women at the 2nd Annual Women's Spiritual Retreat. Nervous and excited, I was prepared to share my personal journey of spiritual awakening. It all felt so surreal.

During the lunch break, I noticed the energy in the room felt particularly heavy from the morning sessions led by other presenters. Trusting my intuition, I grabbed my sage spray and began walking down each aisle of chairs, gently clearing the space. As I did, I called in Archangel Michael to bring in light and protection, asking him to lift the energy and restore balance.

To raise the vibration even further, I pressed play on Justin Timberlake's *"Can't Stop the Feeling"*—and just like that, the room began to shift.

As the women shuffled in, one woman came up front and danced to the music with me. I could feel the space come alive—it was palpable. My heart began to race—I was ready.

When I stepped up to the microphone to begin speaking, something magical happened.

My voice flowed naturally, rising and falling with the rhythm of the story. The women were fully engaged, leaning in, fully immersed in the story. As I discussed my forgiveness journey with my mother, I shared a picture of her and me catching raindrops in our mouths— in the audience tears began to fall freely.

The feedback afterward was extraordinary—many people shared heartfelt testimonials that were truly humbling. I realized then that one of my life's purposes was to be an inspirational speaker.

But wait a minute—*me*, an inspirational speaker?

I believed my purpose was to be a Reiki teacher, psychic, life coach, and death doula. That alone felt like a huge leap. But something deeper began to unfold. My purpose started blossoming into something more—something bigger. I began to feel I was meant to touch lives on a greater scale, to inspire, to serve, and maybe even to reach millions.

It seems like just yesterday that I was a sales representative, fully expecting to retire in that career. But the Universe had other plans. Seemingly overnight, I stepped onto a completely different path—one rooted in healing, intuition, and service.

Speaking at this retreat showed me that more was possible. My calling was expanding to include inspiring others—all of which began with simple videos I posted on social media. I now have a vision of speaking at live venues all over the world.

And now—here I am, an author, writing a book... sharing my story, my truth, and the magic that's been unfolding all along.

How did I evolve from an anxious girl with low self-esteem into a woman rooted in spiritual healing and soul work? How did I find the courage to follow my heart and step onto a path that led me to my truest self?

This is the journey I will share with you in these pages.

First, ask yourself honestly: *Are you at a point in your life where something has to change?*

Do you feel stuck, unfulfilled, or disconnected from your purpose?

Are you yearning for more—but unsure how to take the next step?

I wrote this book to offer not only inspiration, but also a pathway—a way to reconnect with your inner wisdom and begin creating the life you truly desire.

The key is this: stay open to all possibilities.

Because that's where the transformation begins.

That's where you'll discover the magic inside you.

Follow the Yellow Brick Road

"You've always had the power, my dear, you just had to learn it for yourself."
—Glinda, the Good Witch

Dorothy's journey in *The Wizard of Oz* (1939) is a powerful metaphor. Her companions—the Tin Man, the Scarecrow, the Cowardly Lion, and Glinda—were her mentors. They were her guides to finding her way "home," a journey of self-discovery.

Our true destination is a return to deep, unconditional love for ourselves. When we arrive there, we uncover a greater purpose—one rooted in truth and authenticity. From this place, we begin to create a more meaningful and fulfilling life.

Like Dorothy in *The Wizard of Oz*, we often place our faith in something—or someone—outside of ourselves. Dorothy believed the Wizard held the answers, only to discover he was just a man behind a curtain. Her true power had been within her all along.

And so it is with us.

If you're searching for happiness outside of yourself—through material things, validation, or external success—it may satisfy you, but only temporarily.

Home is not a place on a map. It's a place within.

It's the moment you fall in love with yourself as you are—*perfectly imperfect*—and embrace your worth, your light, your wholeness.

On your spiritual journey, you'll cross paths with many souls. Some will become mentors, others may appear for only a moment—but each will play a part in guiding you closer to the unconditional love that lives inside of you.

The Wizard is within you.

You are the change.

You are the powerful creator of your own life.

And now, it's time to begin.

Follow the Signs

"Coincidences are not accidents, but signals from the Universe which can guide us toward our true destiny."
–Deepak Chopra

As I navigated my spiritual path, I discovered that paying attention to signs and synchronicities always validated my deepest decisions. Self-doubt gradually dissolved, replaced by an emerging sense of faith and trust. One of the most important pieces of advice I can give you is to look for the synchronicities. Spirit will show you the path to take—if you look and listen.

One unexpected part of my journey came through an extraordinary woman, a pioneering female hot air balloon pilot from Statesville, North Carolina. In a male-dominated sport, she had carved her own path, becoming Statesville's most celebrated pilot. In 1984, she established AeroSports, Inc., which is now the longest-running, woman-owned, full-service hot air balloon company in the country.

When I met Marsha, I was struck by her calm, humble presence. Yet, there was a strength and beauty to her—one that I imagine has touched many who have been privileged to take a ride with her in her hot air balloon.

In 2009, Warner Brothers approached Marsha with a unique tribute.

They designed a one-of-a-kind hot air balloon featuring *The Wizard of Oz* characters and the iconic ruby red shoes. This marked their 70th-anniversary celebration. Her balloon toured the United States, making nine stops. Along the way, she met five of the original Munchkins, adding magic to an already extraordinary journey.

And then it happened. She offered to take me on a ride in her hot air balloon! I am terrified of heights—a fear we surprisingly shared. Yet, she reassured me that the basket would feel different. As we ascended, tears welled in my eyes.

Surrounded by rolling landscapes, her crew member identified each mountain, and I gleamed with joy. The wind guided us to our final destination—a backyard on private property. The children screamed with excitement, running outside to greet us in their pajamas, followed by their parents. Despite living in Statesville for years—the second-largest hub of hot air ballooning in the country—this was their first encounter with a hot air balloon.

The hot air balloon imagery also held personal significance for me. For years, I had guided people through energy healing journeys using visualization—imagining a ride in a hot air balloon. This technique, often referred to as the "elevator technique," encourages you to visualize your consciousness rising upward, helping you access higher states of being and intuitive wisdom.

Once again, I learned that this was no coincidence. It became the sign for my move to Statesville.

After a few months in my mobile home, I received guidance that it was time to move. My soul was craving the energy of the trees and mountains. So I packed my car and made my way to the Carolinas.

My first stop was in Greenville, South Carolina, where I enjoyed its beautiful stores and restaurants. I then stopped in a tiny town called Traveler's Rest, more fondly known as TR. As I walked the Swamp Rabbit Trail—a path for bikers and walkers—I felt an immense sense of peace. There was something special about this place. You will later learn that this was no coincidence.

The next morning, I awoke to Spirit quietly saying the name "Joanne" in my ear. She was a friend of my best friend in Arizona. I asked him for her number, we connected, and I jumped in my car, heading to North Carolina to meet her for dinner.

I was guided to stop in Statesville for lunch, and afterward, I took a walk, admiring the town's quaint charm. Then, I headed to Mooresville to meet Joanne. With some time before dinner, I strolled down Main Street, visiting a few shops along the way.

I bumped into a lovely couple who were curious about my journey. The wife handed me a business card, and to my surprise, they owned a hot air balloon business in Statesville.

I simply couldn't ignore this sign. And while my move didn't happen immediately, I relocated to Statesville in July of 2024.

What Is a Spiritual Awakening?

"The greatest revelation is that you are not who you think you are."
– Eckhart Tolle

A spiritual awakening is when you recognize that you are more than your personal identity, more than your physical body—it's a connection to something greater than yourself.
What are the signs of a spiritual awakening?

- You are ready to let go of any emotional baggage and traumas attached to past experiences.
- You may feel disconnected from your old beliefs and have a desire to develop a deeper purpose in your life.
- Ultimately, you seek to become more authentic in every area of your life.

It's important to understand that a spiritual awakening is a process, not a destination. It's an ongoing journey that unfolds in stages and layers, offering tremendous self-discovery, healing, and growth.

It usually begins with a triggering event—a life changing moment such as an illness or heartbreak. It can also be a period of deep questioning and reflection, when you grapple with your life's purpose, personal identity, freedom, or mortality.

Ultimately, you will begin to question your past choices, your relationships, and societal conditioning. Emotional healing will bring suppressed emotions, self-limiting beliefs, and traumas to the surface. Old relationships will fade, while new connections will emerge—ones aligned with your growth.

Your priorities will shift, and material possessions will hold far less importance. You will feel more connected to the universe and experience a heightened awareness of your intuition and the synchronicities guiding your path.

It's not all rainbows and unicorns, but you will discover a part of yourself you never knew existed. As you release your old identity, you will tap into **your magic.**

An Invitation to Grow

"Pain is a gift. Pain is your call to action. It's there to wake you up and to move you forward."
— Tony Robbins

An invitation to grow—how profound is that?!

You may be here because you feel that pain, you feel that need for change—and that means you're feeling an invitation to grow. You can transform and discover your inner strength, and I'm here to help you do that.

There is a psychological phenomenon called the 'fresh start effect' where people feel a boost of motivation to make changes in their lives. This generally occurs with a catalyst: the New Year, a birthday, or major life transitions.

Have you thought about what your catalyst might be? Perhaps it's something simple—maybe even something I've mentioned already, like a birthday. But if you dig deep, think about what lies behind it. Why do you feel like it's time to start your journey, your growth, your change?

Don't think about where you want to be or where you think you're going at this stage. It might sound counterintuitive, but focus on the negatives—decide what you want to leave behind, what you want to change. This is a necessary part of the process because otherwise, you'll struggle to let go of old habits that are holding you back.

These milestone moments, these catalysts, help you separate from your past failures. This is the moment you have that real conversation with yourself. This starts with honest self-reflection. The first step is self-awareness. Literally put a name to how you feel. It might be depression, anxiety, career dissatisfaction, or unfulfilled relationships. Allow yourself to cry and truly be vulnerable.

I invite you to take a moment of deep reflection.

Ask yourself:

"Am I willing to change and commit to myself, no matter how painful the process may be?"

This moment is one where you have to be brutally honest with yourself. You are going to enter a zone of uncertainty, and it will be uncomfortable and messy at times. You are making a decision to make yourself a priority and commit fully to changing every aspect of your life.

This isn't selfish. It's a powerful act of self-love and respect. Prioritizing yourself doesn't mean neglecting your role as a partner, professional, or parent. It's about managing your time and energy in a way that includes caring for yourself as much as you care for others. Most importantly, stay committed and be consistent. Trust that every small step, as insignificant as it might seem, contributes to your growth.

What steps will you take toward achieving your goal? This is where you have to identify what you want and why. This means understanding what you are passionate about and what makes your heart sing. I believe you have to love what you do and do what you love.

Now that you have clarified what you want, ask yourself why.

The "why" is the motivation, the thing that puts fire under your feet. This emotion is what ultimately drives your purpose. Do one thing each day to get closer to what you want. Every action has to align with your desires, and it's important to be consistent. Look at the gap between where you are currently and where you want to be.

The key is not to ask "how" or "when." This is where you allow it to unfold organically—to let go and not control it. Your actions will speak loudly to the Universe.

It's important not to be in waiting mode. This tells the Universe that something is missing, and reflects a feeling of lack. Believe that you have everything you need right now, and that the best is yet to come.

The key is this: Stay present and choose joy.

Each day, pick one thing—just one—that makes you feel good. Whether it's a walk in nature, a favorite song, or a quiet moment with tea, let it lift your spirit." Remember, happy people do things that make them happy.

This simple practice raises your vibration, and when your vibration rises, so does your ability to attract abundance, love, and alignment.

Lastly, find a role model. Who inspires you? You do not have to reinvent the wheel. Read their books, watch their YouTube videos, and go to their seminars. You will learn their methods and techniques and create your own unique "recipe" for your deeper purpose, adding your own personal touch to it.

What Was My Catalyst?

"And once the storm is over, you won't remember how you made it through...But one thing is certain. When you come out of the storm, you won't be the same person who walked in."
- Haruki Murakami

In 2006, I moved from Maine to Arizona with my partner of 10 years. In August of 2013, we traveled to Alaska for her fiftieth birthday. Her brother was going through a messy divorce at the time, and it was clear she was questioning her own happiness.

As we entered Denali National Park, she looked at me and said, "I don't want to be with you anymore."

I felt like the air had been sucked out of me. I was utterly devastated. And yet, there we were, with a week's worth of travel still ahead of us. As we hiked through the magnificent landscape of mountains, surrounded by grizzly bears, otters, sea lions, and crumbling glaciers, I made the best of the trip, somehow knowing everything would work out.

When we returned home, I quickly packed my bag and flew to Boston to visit my mother. Meanwhile, something about my partner's behavior didn't sit right. She seemed distracted, her attention focused on someone she had recently friended on Facebook.

While in Boston, my instincts told me something was off. I texted her to check in, and she mentioned that she was attending a Phoenix Mercury basketball game.

I asked her who she was with. "No one," she replied. I knew she was lying.

Pressing her further, she finally admitted the truth later that day. She had flown in a former girlfriend—this new Facebook friend—from Florida. I fell to the floor in tears, my heart ripped from my chest by her betrayal and deception.

Little did I know that this breakup would propel me on a journey beyond anything I could have ever imagined. In hindsight, the end of the relationship was an extraordinary gift from the Universe.

This marked the beginning of my spiritual awakening.

I realized that I needed to change something deep inside of me and that traditional therapy was not the right path. So, I asked the Universe to bring me a teacher.

Not long after, I was invited to a brunch where the hostess gifted all the attendees a psychic reading. The moment I met the psychic, I knew she was meant to be my guide.

How did I know? It was a gut feeling, which was quickly validated once I began studying with her. Her psychic readings on the guests were all romantically centered. With me, it was quite different.

When she did the reading with me, the psychic was able to tap into a man who died in his late twenties. She said he was thanking me for saving his life. I couldn't imagine who this could be. She told me to wait, that it would come to me in a couple of days.

Indeed, it did.

My career began as a Behavior Specialist, working in a locked psychiatric unit in New Hampshire. At first, I worked as a mental health worker on the floor to gain experience with the patients. While working on the admissions unit, we admitted a young man named Michael, with sandy blonde hair, who was battling anorexia. For some reason, I felt drawn to him and volunteered to work with him one-on-one during my shifts. His frailty was alarming, and his feet were so thin that the skin was nearly exposing bone. Fearing for his life, I went to the head nurse and shared my concerns. Michael was moved to the third-floor therapeutic unit, where they hoped he might do better.

One day, when I came in for my shift, I learned he had gone into kidney failure and died. I collapsed in tears.

I realized that the psychic had connected with Michael. I could feel the pain of my efforts with the head nurses, urging them that his situation was critical. I felt an overwhelming sense of gratitude for her connection with him, as my work at the psychiatric hospital was a significant chapter in my career.

Her connection with him played an important role in my decision to choose her as my first teacher. As we began working together weekly, I started noticing improvements in both my physical and mental well-being.

Finding a Teacher, Energy Worker, and/or Mentor

"When the student is ready, the teacher will appear."
-Buddha

Why do you need to work with someone to do the healing work? Because you simply cannot do it alone.

Throughout my life, I have had many teachers and healers who were instrumental in changing my life. Each teacher approached me in their own unique way, providing me with new solutions. Remember, the beauty of our healing journey is that it is ongoing—a process of discovery and transformation.

A teacher will help you on many levels. Pain clouds our vision, and teachers help us see the meaning of our experiences so that we can gain more clarity. Part of this is due to blind spots—the parts of ourselves buried deep in the subconscious. Teachers tend to be unbiased and not partial to our experiences. Thus, they can point out our triggers so that we can begin to heal them.

A teacher also offers a safe, non-judgmental space where they act as a witness. They listen with compassion, remaining neutral and without imposing their own narrative. This allows you to express yourself freely, without fear of being vulnerable.

Remember, the teacher is not here to "fix" you. They are simply facilitators. You have to do the work. They hold you accountable—to be consistent with your spiritual practices, to stay focused, and to remain committed. Through their guidance and wisdom, they support you emotionally as you unravel the parts of yourself that no longer serve you.

When you choose to do energy work with a teacher, it takes you to a deeper level of healing required to unblock stagnant energy, opening you up to receive in new ways. The heart chakra, for example, is where love, compassion, and forgiveness reside. By opening this chakra, we begin the process of self-forgiveness, become more self-loving, and transform our essence.

Where can you find a teacher and energy worker? Network with your spiritual community and attend MeetUp events—get recommendations. Do an internet search, keeping in mind that working virtually is just as effective as in-person. Identify your needs, and once you narrow down a few options, ask if you can schedule a free consultation.

How do you choose your teacher? It starts with following your intuition—an inner knowing. Here are some things to ask yourself:

- Does their energy feel authentic and grounded?
- Do their teachings or energy work align with your values?
- How do you feel around them—empowered or drained?
- Do they practice ethically and approach their work with integrity?
- Do you feel a sense of trust and connection with them?
- What do their testimonials say?
- What is their background and training?
- Does their teaching style resonate with you?

Every person who has come to work with me always says, "I saw you on social media, and I was drawn to you." I do a clarity call with almost every client before they book a session to ensure alignment—not only for them but for me as well.

Tune into the energy of your teacher, and pay attention to how it resonates with you. As you work with them, notice if there is progress. If you begin to feel stuck or stagnant, this may be a sign that it's time to move on to another teacher.

A Course in Miracles: The Shift from Fear to Love

"You cannot be lonely if you like the person you're alone with. The only way to shift from fear to love is to learn to love yourself."
- Wayne Dyer

For nearly three years, I worked closely with my first psychic teacher, studying *A Course in Miracles*. The teachings spoke to my soul, and I immersed myself in the daily reading and lessons. We met weekly at first, and each time, she cleared and balanced my chakras and provided me with guidance. It was painful, difficult work, and so many emotions came up from my past. However, I made the choice to work through it, and in the end, it changed my life.

Some of you may not be familiar with *A Course in Miracles* (ACIM). It is a self-study spiritual text designed to guide readers toward inner peace and understanding through the principles of forgiveness, shifting fear to love. Written by Dr. Helen Schucman and her colleague Dr. William Thetford in the 1960s, it is said to be inspired by what Schucman described as a divine inner voice she identified as Jesus.

The text's core principles center on the belief that love is the only true reality and that everything else is an illusion. It emphasizes forgiveness as the path to peace, defining miracles as fundamental shifts in perception from fear to love. ACIM explores how to deconstruct the ego—a false sense of self rooted in fear and separation—and reveals a profound interconnectedness where all beings share a common divine essence.

My personal belief is that a teacher is essential in interpreting this book.

Working one-on-one with my first spiritual teacher was a profound turning point in my journey. Through her guidance, I experienced layers of healing I never thought possible. Her methods—ranging from energy work and cord-cutting to deep inner exploration—created a sacred space where I could finally release old wounds and experience the transformative power of forgiveness, both for myself and for others.

During this time, I learned to meditate and journal and cultivate other methods for healing. This "spiritual toolkit" became the foundation of my transformation, a means to create a new version of myself. I was "unbecoming" who I was, shedding the layers of pain and limiting beliefs that no longer served me.

Forgiveness, of myself and others, became a cornerstone of my journey. In forgiving myself, I opened my heart to truly accept and love who I was. I replaced the anger and resentment I felt toward those who had hurt me with gratitude, recognizing that my experiences with them were profound opportunities for growth and transformation.

I'm not going to lie—there were days when I felt completely lost. Depressed. Anxious. Without direction.

There were moments when I questioned everything—when I felt hopeless, overwhelmed, and found myself in tears with no clear reason why.

What got me through was my unwavering commitment to myself. My anchor was my daily spiritual practice of journaling, meditating, and deep self-care.

I am forever grateful for the weekly meetings with my mentor—her wisdom and guidance kept me grounded when I felt like giving up.

But here's the truth. I refused to quit on myself. No matter how heavy it got, I persevered.

My words of wisdom to you. Keep going. Don't give up.

The path of healing is long, and it takes great patience. But I promise you this.

Every moment of pain you endure will open something beautiful and profound inside of you—something you never knew was there. I wrote many poems during this time, and this is one that I wanted to share with you:

Where I Belong
Each foot gently sinks into the sand.
Darkness blinding me
The sound of breaking waves
Gently guide me
To the water's edge.
As it gently washes over my feet,
Tingles of joy dance
Inside of me.
As I walk down the beach,
The clouds clear, and
A full moon appears.
A light drizzle of rain
Gently kisses my face
Fond memories of
Jumping in puddles
Warm my chilled body.
The child inside of me
Still alive.
My wrinkles
Slightly show my years.
And yet ever so softly
All fear is gone
The present moment
Embracing me
Loving me

Beyond any spoken word
I have ever heard.
It all makes sense.
Every hardship
Every tear
Etched their path
To here.
To now.
The place where
I belong.

Lisa Bromfield
7/28/2014

Three years into my studies, I attended my teacher's seminar, "How to Build Intuition and Psychic Abilities." I joked with her beforehand, saying, "Me, psychic? I don't think so!" But three weeks into the class, something shifted. I tapped into my psychic abilities.

I am infinitely grateful to this teacher. Through her guidance, I healed countless wounds and embarked on an unimaginable journey. My new path was in front of me now, and little did I realize that I would soon step into my calling as a full-time psychic, medium, and energy healer.

I would meet my second teacher at a Meetup group hosted at a local crystal store in Tempe, Arizona. After class, she approached me and shared that she ran a psychic and mediumship development group at her home. She encouraged me to attend, so I thought I would give it a try.

On my first Saturday session, I joined a small group of four to practice psychic readings using oracle cards. Her son was part of the group, and as we were working, he turned to his mom and said, "This gal is really gifted," referring to me!

Before he could even finish his words, she nodded and said, "I know."

She believed in me from the start and took me under her wing as a mentor. I continued to attend the Saturday groups, which gave me the opportunity to interact with as many as twenty other people, all focused on developing their psychic abilities. Her support and guidance helped build my confidence and deepen my connection to Spirit.

She also hosted a once-a-month psychic fair at her home and invited me to be one of the readers. This experience was invaluable, as it allowed me to work one-on-one with people rather than in a group. I was thrilled to see that, month after month, some of the same individuals returned for a reading with me. Their trust in my abilities boosted my confidence and validated that I was truly on the right path.

It was only through surrendering and passing through the negativity of the heartbreak that came with it that I was able to open the door to this whole new level of spiritual connection.

Stepping Into My Calling

"Courage doesn't always roar. Sometimes courage is the quiet voice at the end of the day saying, 'I will try again tomorrow.'"
—Mary Anne Radmacher

As I evolved through immense change with my teachers, it became clear I would have to let go of my sales career. I was not happy with my job—in fact, I was miserably bored! Since I did not have the courage to quit, the Universe, in its infinite wisdom, delivered the hypothetical two-by-four to manage this!

Spirit sent me a clear message that my job would soon come to an end. When I shared this insight with my boss, he dismissed it, insisting that my position was secure and that I would retire in my sales role.

Three months later, I was called in for my annual review. I learned my sales position had indeed been eliminated.

I cried at first, and then I experienced an immense sense of relief. It felt like a burden had been lifted off my shoulders. While the responsibility of owning a home with a mortgage and no job felt overwhelming at first, I knew I had to trust and have faith in the process.

My next steps were clear: it was time to officially open my private practice as a psychic, medium, energy healer, and life coach. Although I had no prior experience building a website, I dove in headfirst.

After two weeks of intense focus and pure determination, my website was ready to launch. I created business cards, ready to embrace the new chapter of my life.

Shortly after, I built a shamanic drum. Interestingly, I had been listening to a drumming meditation online and noticed how the rhythmic sound of the drum put me in an altered state of consciousness.

Trusting the guidance, I began an internet search that led me to a nearby shaman, who agreed to help me build a drum. We set a date, and, keeping with tradition, he soaked the elk skin overnight to prepare it to be wrapped around the drum's frame. Then he, his medicine-woman wife, and I worked together at the table, weaving her into existence. Once completed, he cleansed her with palo santo.

I decided to name my drum "Serena," as she has brought me tremendous peace. I have integrated her not only into my private sessions with clients but also into my work as a death doula. She has always been well received, and her medicine truly has been a gift to me and others.

To this day, all of my private clients work with me virtually. This has allowed me to touch lives globally. As you will see next, my journey with social media unfolded in exactly the same way.

Follow the Universe's Plan

> *"Follow your bliss and the Universe will open doors where there were only walls."*
> *-Joseph Campbell*

On July 30, 2020, my birthday, I received a video message on Facebook Messenger from a complete stranger in Phoenix. This made the birthday wish even more meaningful. I knew this was a sign.

Spirit whispered gently in my ear, "Your mission is to start creating inspirational videos on Facebook." I was taken aback.

Not being active on social media, I responded, "Are you kidding me?" But Spirit was not joking.

The world was hibernating in fear due to COVID, and people were craving physical and emotional connection.

Following the nudge, I began posting videos the next day, listening to my inner guidance and crafting each message to inspire and uplift the collective. I started on Facebook but soon expanded to Instagram and YouTube. I learned that two key factors in success were keeping the videos under a minute long and posting them consistently.

My social media followers responded by sharing replies and private messages that touched my heart. The videos, while short, had a great impact on their lives. Something special was happening.

This endeavor also became a source of a steady stream of clients for my private practice. I learned that I did not have to "chase" business. Simply showing up authentically was enough to attract clients who resonated with my energy. The law of attraction was in play!

During this time, I had a Quantum Human Design reading done to understand myself on a deeper level. This system, developed by Karen Curry Parker, helps align you with your true purpose. It combines astrology, the I Ching, the Kabbalah, the chakra system, and quantum physics to create a personalized blueprint for self-discovery and transformation. There are five energy types: Manifestor, Generator, Manifesting Generator, Projector, and Reflector.

I learned that I am a Projector and that my work on social media was perfectly aligned with this type. My role as a Projector, simply put, was to be a teacher and guide. Intuitively, I was already embodying this purpose, and the reading provided powerful validation that I was on the right path.

If you are interested in learning more about your Human Design, visit www.quantumhumandesign.com. You can also do an internet search for someone who offers these readings or look on YouTube.

It's important to find someone educated in all areas of Human Design due to its complexity. It not only shows you how to live in alignment with your design but also helps you create more harmonious relationships and identify the career path that will best fulfill your life's purpose.

What is Spirit, Our Higher Self, and our Guides?

"There is a voice that doesn't use words. Listen."
— Rumi

What does it mean when I say, 'Spirit spoke to me'? And how did I learn to listen?

First of all, it's not necessarily a voice. It's often a gentle nudge... a gut feeling I simply couldn't ignore. Sometimes, the messages came through during my daily meditations. Other times, they arrived through signs and synchronicities that felt too aligned to be coincidence. It was my heart quietly saying, *"This is the way."*

You don't need to be a psychic or a healer to hear Spirit. You may refer to Spirit as something else—Source, your Higher Self, or your Guides.

Your guides are the unseen energy walking beside you through every step of your journey. They may come as ancestors, angels, or beings of light—each one here to support you, protect you, and gently guide you home to yourself... home to love. They speak through signs, synchronicities, dreams, and quiet stirrings within your heart.

What is your Higher Self?

It's the part of you that holds your soul's truth—your infinite wisdom. The most divine, whole, and loving version of you. Your Higher Self isn't outside of you or separate from you. It *is* you.

The essence of you—beyond the fear, the doubt, and the noise. The guide within that always leads you back to love.

In my private sessions, I help clients connect with their Higher Self. Sometimes, they appear as their younger self. Other times, older. And sometimes just as they are now. I invite the client into stillness and ask them to trust the message they receive from their Higher Self in that sacred silence.

And without fail—every client receives something beautiful. Because we *all* have the ability to connect with this divine presence within us. We just have to slow down... listen... and remember.

It's easier than you think to connect with your inner guidance. All it takes is a little quiet, a little trust, and a willingness to listen. Your heart already knows the way home.

At first, I didn't trust the voice of my Higher Self. I second-guessed everything. Honestly, I drove myself a little crazy. But the key—my turning point—was learning to slow down enough to really listen.

My journey into spiritual work didn't begin with a lightning bolt or a loud calling. It began with restlessness. A subtle ache. A sense that I was meant for something more. Sometimes the messages were clear. Other times, the Universe left breadcrumbs—small signs and soft guidance—urging me to take one step at a time.

Here's what helped me strengthen my connection to Spirit:

- Silence — Spirit speaks loudest when the world is quiet.
- Journaling — Writing helped me receive and trust the messages.
- Reiki & Meditation — These opened the energetic channels and deepened my awareness.
- Nature — Spirit is everywhere, but I hear Her clearest among the trees, the wind, and the water.
- Trusting the small things — When I acted on the little nudges, they led

me to bigger truths.

We are *all* intuitive and "psychic."

The messages can come to you through what are known as the Clairs—distinct forms of intuitive perception that go beyond the five physical senses. These are your *spiritual senses* where you receive divine guidance and insight. You access your inner magic through your Clairs! Think of them as the sacred gifts you were born with—always within you, simply waiting for you to be open and receive.

Here's a breakdown of the most commonly known Clairs that I explain to my clients:

1. **Clairvoyance (Clear Seeing)** is the ability to see images, symbols, or visions in the mind's eye—or even with the physical eyes—that are not present in the physical world. An example is seeing a spirit or image that isn't physically there, or receiving a visual flash of insight about something in the future.
2. **Clairaudience (Clear Hearing)** is the ability to hear sounds, voices, or messages from the spiritual realm or Higher Self that aren't audible to the physical ears. An example is hearing a voice in your mind or heart that offers you wise guidance or reassurance.
3. **Clairsentience (Clear Feeling or Sensing)** is the ability to sense or feel emotions, physical sensations, or energies of people, places, or situations. An example of this is feeling suddenly anxious or sad without an apparent reason—only to discover you were tuning into someone else's emotions.
4. **Claircognizance (Clear Knowing)** is the ability to just *know* something without any logical explanation. This insight comes as an inner knowing that feels undeniable. An example is instantly knowing the answer to a question or having a sudden, intuitive understanding of a person or situation.
5. **Clairalience (Clear Smelling)** is the ability to smell scents that aren't physically present, often associated with spirits or loved ones who've

passed. An example is smelling your grandmother's perfume or the familiar scent of a loved one who's no longer here.

These Clairs represent the many ways we can receive guidance beyond the physical senses—deepening our connection to intuition, spirit, and healing. They can be nurtured through meditation, mindfulness, and sacred spiritual practices.

The Journey with TikTok

"The more you trust yourself, the more amazing opportunities will come your way."
—Shakti Gawain

I had been hesitant about joining TikTok, mostly because the content seemed silly, and I wasn't sure it would align with my messages about spiritual awakening.

Then Spirit spoke up again, loud and clear, "Get on TikTok."

Trusting the guidance, I decided to give it a chance. I began posting videos and doing live streams. To my surprise, the TikTok audience was engaging, vibrant, and full of energy. I found myself looking forward to the live streams, purely for the joy of connecting with others.

I had no expectations from the platform, yet every time I went live, more private bookings came through. My following steadily grew, and my heart swelled with gratitude as I realized I was reaching and touching more lives than ever before.

The Universe was showering me with abundance—not just through appointments but also in the heartfelt feedback from those attending the live streams. People commented on how they could "feel" my energy and that my very presence brought them a sense of peace and comfort.

I realized a profound truth: The energy people felt from me, both online and in person, was love. I now understand that love is our superpower.

As a channel for pure, unconditional love, I embody a truth that can inspire and transform others. As energetic beings, distance does not matter. We are all connected as one.

On my live streams, I began to speak about the "ripple effect." I would tell the audience, "If you feel better after this live stream, then your higher vibration will impact those directly or indirectly in your energy field."

Left to my own devices, I might have dismissed TikTok as trivial, but I had faith in the guidance from Spirit and went with it.

Stop ignoring the "feelings" and signs. Let go of the doubt and fear. Take the leap of faith. Decide to listen.

Your decision will change your life.

At times, you won't know where the path is leading you—the key is to plant the seeds, try something out of your comfort zone, and see what gains traction. If it grows, keep going. If it doesn't, pivot and try something else.

Because I trusted the nudge to get on TikTok, another magical opportunity arrived. One night, just as I was about to end a livestream, I received a clear and unexpected message from Spirit:

"Ask for a t-shirt sponsor."

It felt random—and yet, I knew better. What is interesting is that I am always searching for t-shirts with meaningful messages. So, I followed the guidance… and what unfolded next was in pure alignment.

Without hesitation, I voiced the request, and magically, the sponsor appeared. She responded in the comments that she would be in touch with me.

The next day, I connected with the owner, Janice. She told me that she and her husband ran a t-shirt business out of their basement, charmingly named "Goat Dog Tees." Intrigued, I looked up the symbolic meaning of the goat as a spirit animal:

Goat symbolism often signifies the start of new climbs and endeavors. It's a reminder to plan carefully and take your time, ensuring you are sure footed on your journey. Like the Mountain Goat, it encourages you to stretch yourself and aim for higher goals.

This resonated deeply with me, as it perfectly mirrored the growth and expansion I was experiencing.

Janice and I spoke on the phone and shared ideas about the messaging on the t-shirts. Her husband had access to wonderful design programs, and they immediately went to work. Within a few weeks, they shipped me some shirts, and I snapped some photos of myself wearing them in the park. I became the model for the t-shirts on Shopify. My audience loved seeing the shirts in action!

The captions on the T-shirts included:

- Have a Terrific Day (the tagline on all of my videos)
- Have Only Positive Expectations
- Love is Our Super Power
- You Are Magic
- Gratitude is the Best Attitude
- An Infinity Sign with "To Infinity and Beyond"

These t-shirts weren't just apparel—they carried beautiful, intentional messages. I've always understood the power of words, and wearing these shirts was another way to spread love and positivity.

On my daily walks, it was always a delight when someone stopped to comment on the message printed on my shirt. These small moments of connection reinforced a growing awareness within me: I was being prepared for something much bigger.

Embracing the Journey

"Nothing ever goes away until it has taught us what we need to know."
-Pema Chodron

I've had my share of challenges along the way—doubts, fears, and moments when I wasn't sure if I was on the right path to stepping into my true purpose.

Let's take a moment to recognize and validate the shared obstacles we face as we heal and transform our lives. It's completely normal for a range of emotions to surface—this is simply part of unraveling old conditioning and healing the deeper parts of ourselves.

I encourage you to embrace your journey with grace and without judgment, knowing that you're opening your heart to new and beautiful experiences.

As you move forward, you will undoubtedly feel some negative emotions. This is to be expected. It doesn't mean it "isn't working" or that this path isn't right for you. It simply means you're working through difficult feelings. You may experience anxiety, depression, and exhaustion. There will be days when you wake up feeling lost, spinning, with no clear direction. You'll have to confront the painful parts of your life that you've created and take responsibility for them. But through this process, you'll begin to release what no longer serves you and step into a new chapter—one aligned with who you truly are. Let's dive even deeper.

Abandonment

"You are loved just for being who you are, just for existing."
- Ram Dass

Do you sometimes feel lonely, discarded, unlovable, and left behind? Do you feel flawed and unfixable?

We have all been there. I believe that abandonment issues are at the core of much of our healing.

The feeling of abandonment penetrates us to the core. When our parents are not present for us, it leaves us feeling unsafe. These wounds of emotional neglect and betrayal of trust create patterns that echo throughout our adult relationships.

This manifests in various ways, such as people-pleasing or pushing people away. It can also show up as fierce independence or co-dependence—attaching to one or both extremes, unable to find a healthy balance. Abandonment is also a key aspect of healing the inner child. It requires addressing the betrayal and deception we felt as children that left us feeling "unlovable" and "not enough."

You will begin to notice what triggers this feeling of abandonment. It can be as simple as someone not responding to a text or email. Notice it, acknowledge it, and feel it—to heal it.

As you heal, you will begin to develop trust again. The false narratives in your mind will slowly dissipate. You will build a new sense of empowerment, recognizing that you are worthy and that you are enough.

You will be tested, and sometimes an old fear will resurface. However, as you heal abandonment issues, you will be better prepared each time you face them in a situation or relationship. You will be able to express your needs more clearly, set healthy boundaries, and approach all connections differently.

You are building a stronger relationship with yourself so that nothing can disturb your inner peace.

What Is Self-Love?

~~~~~

"To love oneself is the beginning of a lifelong romance."
— Oscar Wilde

One of the core messages of this book is learning how to "fall in love" with yourself. Self-love is the practice of caring for yourself with kindness, compassion, and acceptance—regardless of your flaws, mistakes, or imperfections. It means recognizing your own worth, honoring your needs, and nurturing your well-being—emotionally, physically, and spiritually.

Self-love isn't about being narcissistic or self-centered; it's about acknowledging your inherent value and treating yourself with the same compassion you would offer a loved one.

Loving yourself unconditionally—through every thought, word, and action—shapes the way you relate to both yourself and others. When you truly practice self-love, you begin to thrive in every aspect of life.

My mother's critical and demeaning words created a deep sense of unworthiness within me. I hated myself for not being enough. I believed that if I could just gain her approval, I would finally feel worthy of her love.

I spent hours cleaning the house, making sure the vacuum left perfect, symmetrical patterns in the carpet. I carefully organized her closet, lining up every shoe. My efforts—sincere and meticulous—never seemed to earn the love I so desperately craved.

And so, her gift of rejection became the very path that led me to learn how to love myself unconditionally.

Remember this: **Don't live in your story.** It does not define you. The rejection you feel is not a reflection of your worth. It is forging your strength and resilience—and that courage will carry you to the love you deserve within yourself.

Inner Child Work

> *"The healed inner child becomes a source of vitality and creativity,*
> *enabling us to find new joy and energy in living."*
> —John Bradshaw

An unhealed inner child can manifest in many ways—intense mood swings, repeating negative relationship patterns, difficulty setting boundaries, perfectionism, unresolved anger and resentment, and even physical symptoms.

This all ties back to abandonment. It significantly impacts the relationship you have with yourself and others. As you begin inner child work, you will find it overlaps with what is known as "shadow work." Shadow work is the profound journey of facing the subconscious parts of ourselves that we have learned to repress, deny, or hide. These are the deeply wounded parts of us that reside in the subconscious, making them difficult to explore and heal because of the pain they hold.

This is where trauma and self-limiting beliefs reside. Over many years, we become fragmented due to various traumas. This leads to self-sabotaging patterns—sometimes literally destroying anything good that comes our way.

As we heal through shadow work, we learn unconditional love and compassion for ourselves. We begin to accept our flaws and imperfections, releasing the harsh judgments we have imposed on ourselves for so long.

To heal the inner child, you must first acknowledge the wounded parts of yourself. Recognize that your inner child deserves love and nurturing. As you heal, you will feel more whole, more connected to yourself, and more able to live authentically. Once you have done this, revisit your past—both the painful and the good experiences. Connect with those feelings and how they made you feel back then.

Journaling can be a powerful tool in this process. Write a letter to your inner child, reassuring them that they are safe, loved, and supported. Use your journal as a cathartic practice to release hurt and emotions, expressing anger in a healthy way. Practice using positive affirmations such as "I am safe now," "I am worthy of love," and "I am enough." These can help rebuild a positive self-image and heal old wounds. You are creating your reality as you write these intentions and affirmations.

Consider incorporating your inner child into your meditation practice. Visualize holding them in your lap, hugging them, and offering love. Taking time to practice forgiveness—of yourself and those who hurt you—is essential in healing the inner child. (This will be covered more fully in the next chapter.)

You may have heard of the term "reparenting." Many of us did not receive proper nurturing from our parents. Now, it is our responsibility to be our own parent. This means loving ourselves through every action—self-care, setting healthy boundaries, and practicing self-compassion.

This is heavy work, so it's essential to balance it with playfulness. Grab some art supplies—paint, markers, clay—whatever calls to you—and create freely. Put on music and dance. Let joy move through you. To lighten up my own journey, I remember attending an art class where I dipped my hands and feet in different colored paints and imprinted them all over a huge sheet of white paper. I felt like a kid again—and it was such a wonderful release.

Inner child work is an essential practice for emotional healing and growth. Because it is intense work, I suggest finding the right practitioners to support you through this journey.

The Power of Forgiveness

"To forgive is the highest, most beautiful form of love. In return, you will receive untold peace and happiness."
—Robert Muller

Do you find yourself beating yourself up over past mistakes? Do you dwell on someone who hurt you, constantly revisiting that story? Does the pain go so deep that you simply can't let it go?

The next crucial step in healing, as part of abandonment, is forgiveness. This means forgiving both yourself and those who caused you heartbreak, trauma, and pain.

There's no sugarcoating this—it's painful work.

Forgiveness is like unlocking a ball and chain you've been dragging around your entire life. Through this process, you release guilt, shame, and self-judgment. You let go of the past and the story you've been attached to. As a result, you'll build a healthier relationship with yourself and others.

You are perfectly imperfect. You haven't made mistakes—you've learned some difficult lessons, and this has provided you with an opportunity to grow. The people who hurt you don't need to remain in your life for you to do this work. You might resist forgiveness, thinking that it's impossible or unjust.

A good starting point is this: **Be willing to forgive.**

It's important to understand that forgiving someone doesn't mean condoning their actions. You may not choose to keep this person in your life. Forgiveness is about freeing yourself, not about excusing their behavior.

The final piece of forgiveness is gratitude. Be grateful to those who hurt you. This might seem counterintuitive at first, but this is where you can transform pain into wisdom. By embracing gratitude, you begin to see that these individuals were your teachers, helping you grow with each painful experience.

As a guide and channel for healing, I am continuously moved by the transformative power of forgiveness that I witness in each of my clients. Though it's painful and challenging work, the healing that results is truly life changing.

One of the most profound practices I've experienced with myself and my clients is the practice of Ho'oponopono. This ancient Hawaiian practice, originally used to resolve family conflicts, was revitalized in the twentieth century by Kahuna Morrnah Simeona.

It consists of four simple but powerful phrases:

"I'm sorry. Please forgive me. I love you. I thank you."

This ancient Hawaiian practice of forgiveness functions as both a tool for restoring self-love and balance. As a forgiveness practice, it is also deeply resonant, as it tends to penetrate our inner monologue over time. In practice, it works sort of like a mantra for self-love. And, even more surprisingly, it's super simple.

The word Ho'oponopono roughly translates to "cause things to move back in balance" or to "make things right." It's a very Zen concept. (In the native Hawaiian language, pono means balance, in the sense of life. When things are in balance, nothing is off, so to speak.)

Accordingly, chanting this prayer over and over is a powerful way to cleanse the body of guilt, shame, haunting memories, ill will, or bad feelings that keep the mind fixated on negative thoughts.

When you say, "I'm sorry," to someone who has hurt you, you're not apologizing to them. Instead, by saying, "I'm sorry," you are asking for forgiveness for your own negative thoughts and feelings tied to the situation. This helps release the pain that is associated with it.

The "I'm sorry" in Ho'oponopono isn't about admitting guilt to the other person. Rather, it's about acknowledging that your perception of them has created negativity within you—and you are taking responsibility for clearing that negativity. It's about cleansing your own energy, not changing the other person. This process clears any blocks that prevent you from creating inner peace.

Take time in meditation to chant the Ho'oponopono mantra several times out loud. Keep your eyes closed, and place your left hand on your heart. You can also hold a mirror and look into your eyes as you chant. Feel the words at a deep level, allowing them to dissolve the negative experience.

There are Ho'oponopono meditations on YouTube that can help facilitate this process as well. Find one that resonates with you and use it daily. I sometimes said the mantra several times a day when I felt I needed it.

A powerful method that can be combined with forgiveness work is cord cutting. Let's take some time to explore this.

What is Cord Cutting?

"Forgiveness is the key to inner peace because it is the mental technique by which our thoughts are transformed from fear to love."
—Marianne Williamson

During my work with my first teacher, she performed energetic cord cutting. This was an important part of healing past traumas with my family members. With each session, we would call forward anyone I had not forgiven; sometimes the same people would show up, sometimes different ones. I would rate on a 0-10 scale how I felt about each person that I worked with after we cut the cords. Over time, the numbers reduced to zero, and they no longer showed up in the session.

Cord cutting is a powerful energetic practice used to release unhealthy attachments between yourself and another person, situation, or even a past version of you. These energetic "cords" form through relationships and interactions—especially intense or emotionally charged ones—and can remain long after the connection has ended

Energetic cords are invisible ties that connect your energy field to someone else's. They can be loving and supportive, but when the relationship becomes toxic, co-dependent, or unresolved, these cords can drain your energy, cause emotional distress, and block your spiritual growth.

Cord cutting is the intentional act of releasing these energetic ties to reclaim your power, clear emotional residue, and make space for healing and growth. It doesn't mean you're cutting the person out of your life (unless you choose to); it simply removes the energetic entanglement that no longer serves you. Love always remains; the intention is to remove only the negative connections holding us back from our highest expression.

Why Cord Cutting Is Important on the Spiritual Journey

- Helps release past wounds and emotional baggage
- Frees you from old patterns or toxic dynamics
- Allows you to reclaim your own energy and power
- Creates space for higher vibrational connections
- Enhances your connection to your Higher Self

Common Signs You Might Need to Cut Cords with Someone or a Dynamic

- You are constantly thinking about them
- You feel emotionally drained after interactions
- You're repeating the same relational patterns
- You feel energetically "tied" to a memory or person
- You're having difficulty moving on

When I take private clients into a session, we combine forgiveness work with cord cutting. I use a different method than my teacher originally showed me. There are several steps I take the client through:

1. After clearing and balancing the chakras, I have clients imagine someone with whom they have an attachment that no longer serves them. I then have them imagine the essence of themselves standing in front of the other person. I ask them to feel and imagine energetic cords connected to each of them.

2. I call in Michael the Archangel and have him "pull out" and cut the cords.
3. Then the client recites the Ho'oponopono mantra to begin the self-forgiveness process.
4. We then invite four more people that they need to forgive. Each time, the client feels specific people stepping forward.
5. We repeat the cutting of the cords and the Ho'oponopono mantra.

This part of the session is often deeply emotional—many of my clients cry as they experience the power of release and come to a profound understanding of the true importance of forgiveness. Cord cutting may be needed more than once, depending on the depth of the energetic ties.

Karmic Lessons

"Life is an echo. What you send out comes back. What you sow, you reap. What you give, you get. What you see in others, exists in you."
-Zig Ziglar

Every challenge, every relationship and every experience carry an energetic imprint. Karma is simply energy in motion. It's a reflection of what we put out to the Universe, coming back to us to help us grow and evolve.

Karma is greatly misunderstood and tends to have a negative connotation. People feel it is a punishment, or that they did something wrong. Karma is not bad, it is not to be feared, it is not about suffering.

My karmic lessons have come around my relationships with my family, in particular with my mother and my brothers. I realize that I am here not just to experience the karmic lessons, but to alchemize them—turning my pain, my insight and my healing into medicine for others. Karma is loving, wise, and balanced. It is your soul's way of remembering what it came here to learn.

Karmic lessons are repeated experiences that facilitate growth. They continue to show up until you have learned. They are painful, often heartbreaking experiences—part of "Earth School." When the lesson is complete, you might hear your soul say, "I understand, and I thank you."

How do you recognize karmic patterns? They typically show up in relationships, how we react to stress and fear, and our thinking patterns.

Here's how you can start to work with patterns that seem like they may be karmic.

Contemplate the patterns have you seen repeated in your life:

- In love and relationships?
- In how you speak to yourself?
- In your career or creativity?
- How do you show up when you're afraid?
- What do you allow or tolerate?
- What do you keep avoiding?

Here is an exercise that might be helpful:

- Identify the pattern: What situation, feeling, or person keeps showing up again?

Example: *I keep attracting romantic partners that are not available*

- Explore how it feels: What emotions come up?

Example: *I feel stressed and unworthy.*

- When did it begin? Has it shown up in past relationships or your childhood?

Example: *"I can't let go of what happened. It's who I am now."*

- What is it teaching you?

Once you have worked through this exercise, it's a good time to pull your

journal out and write some positive affirmations. These might include:
"I trust myself to choose differently now."
"I deserve relationships that honor my heart."
"I am breaking cycles and becoming free."

How Do You Know the Karmic Lesson Is Complete?

- **You're No Longer Triggered:** When you think about the person or situation, you feel neutral. There's no anger, guilt, or resentment—just a calm sense of empowerment.
- **The Pattern No Longer Repeats:** The cycle that once showed up again and again has come to a full stop. You've broken the loop.
- **You Feel Genuine Gratitude:** You see the lesson for what it was, recognizing your growth and no longer identifying as a victim. Gratitude naturally arises.
- **You've Forgiven:** You've truly forgiven yourself and others. Blame falls away, and in its place is a deep sense of freedom and release.
- **You Feel Energetically Lighter:** It's as if a heavy weight has been lifted from your heart. You move through life with more ease and lightness.
- **You Hear the Inner Message:** Whether from your guides, Higher Self, or inner knowing—you receive the clear message: *"It is done. You are complete."*

So, I knew my karmic lesson was complete with my mother, as her criticism no longer triggered me. It did not create a reaction. I felt more empowered, and it brought me to the realization of how unhappy my mother was with herself, and that she was simply projecting her unhappiness onto me.

Once you break free from these karmic patterns, your relationships will be more loving and supportive.

Boundaries and Relationships

"Boundaries are a form of self-care. They are the distance at which I can love you and me simultaneously."
—Prentis Hemphill

Who makes you feel comfortable? Who makes you feel drained? Are your relationships out of balance, with you giving more than receiving? Do you have difficulty saying 'no?' Do you feel guilty for prioritizing yourself?

Let's first explore what boundaries actually are, because this is an important topic.

For much of my life, I thought being a "good person" meant being available to everyone—saying yes, helping, giving more even when I was running on empty. I confused self-sacrifice with love. But over time, I realized that real love—*healthy* love—includes boundaries.

Boundaries are not walls to keep people out. They're bridges that help us stay connected without losing ourselves. Learning to listen to Spirit also meant learning to listen to myself—my body, my energy, my intuition. And so often, Spirit would whisper: *That doesn't feel right. You're allowed to say no.*

I didn't grow up knowing how to set boundaries. Like many of us, I learned the hard way—through burnout, heartbreak, overgiving, and resentment. I'd say yes when I meant no. I'd let people drain me because I didn't want to disappoint them. I thought if I just loved harder, they would change. They didn't. But I did.

I've learned to find my voice with my family. Sometimes that means stepping back gently and choosing silence. Other times, it means speaking up and firmly letting them know when something isn't okay. Setting boundaries with family can be one of the most challenging parts of personal growth. Just because they're family doesn't give them permission to treat us poorly.

On my journey, I've discovered that my closest, most nourishing relationships have been with a few true friends—not my family. These friendships became my support system, showing me the power of surrounding myself with people who truly respect and understand me.

So, what *are* boundaries?

Boundaries are the energetic agreements we make with ourselves and others. They're how we teach people how to treat us. They say:

This is what I'm okay with. This is what I'm not. And I can love you without abandoning myself in the process.

In healthy relationships, boundaries sound like:

- I need some time to myself today.
- I'm not available for that right now.
- That doesn't feel respectful to me.
- I love you, but I need to take care of myself first.

Boundaries aren't selfish—they're sacred. They protect our peace, our purpose, and our power.

They create space for honest, soulful connection because we're no longer pretending, people-pleasing, or hiding our truth.

As your confidence grows and your self-esteem begins to rise, settling for less than you deserve becomes non-negotiable. You start to see clearly—what aligns with your truth and what no longer fits. This may mean walking away from a romantic relationship, a friendship, or even certain family members. I call this *spiritual discernment.*

It's not easy. In fact, it can be one of the most painful parts of the healing journey. When you begin honoring your boundaries, not everyone will celebrate you for it. Some will challenge you. Some will take it personally. Some may try to guilt, shame, or manipulate you back into old patterns.

But here's the truth: You are not responsible for how others respond to your growth.

Your job is not to manage their emotions. Your job is to stay true to your own. Yes, you may face confrontation. Yes, it will be uncomfortable. But discomfort is a sign of transformation. This is where you reclaim your power. You may get push back. People may test your boundaries.

Stand in your truth. Be clear. Be consistent. Do not make exceptions. This is how you show yourself—and the Universe—that you are ready to rise.

How Do You Begin to Set Healthy Boundaries?

1. **Know your needs.** Be aware of what makes you feel safe, valued, and at peace. Identify what makes you feel uncomfortable or drained.
2. **Communicate clearly.** Express your boundaries openly and honestly.
3. **Start small.** Set a simple boundary—like limiting time on the phone with someone who overwhelms you. Then, work up to more complex situations.

For me, the journey of setting boundaries began with one of the hardest relationships of my life—my mother.

Admitting the truth to myself was painful, but it was clear. If I continued to live in close proximity to her, it would destroy me. The emotional weight, the patterns, the unspoken expectations—it was too much. So, I created distance the only way I knew how—by moving farther and farther away.

It wasn't out of spite. It was an act of self-preservation. An act of self-love.

Other awakenings came through friendships. I began noticing how certain people made me feel after spending time with them—exhausted, drained, and heavy. These relationships were one-sided. I was giving, and they were taking. The energy exchange was completely out of balance.

I had to be honest with myself: *This isn't what friendship is supposed to feel like.*

The key was learning to listen to my energy. That wave of fatigue or the heavy sigh after a conversation. The tightening in my chest, or that subtle restlessness I couldn't shake. My body was always telling the truth—even when my mind tried to rationalize it away. When I finally reached my limit, I found the strength to step away. I believe we all deserve to be surrounded by people who lift us—who return love, joy, and respect, and who see our light without trying to dim it.

Time for an Exercise: Boundary Audit

List your core values.

- Write down ten values that are most important to you—like honesty, peace, or time.

Evaluate your key relationships.

- Write down the people you interact with the most. Do your boundaries with them reflect your values?

Identify draining situations.

- List moments where you feel resentful, uncomfortable, or depleted. Who or what caused these feelings? How would you like to change that?

Practice "I" Statements: Use these to start expressing boundaries with grace and strength.

- "I need conversations where both of us feel heard."
- "That doesn't work for me."
- "I value this relationship, and I also need space to honor my own growth."

- "I love you, and I also need alone time to feel balanced."

You may have to make a big decision: *Who stays in your life, and who needs to leave?*

For those you choose to step away from, remember—it might be temporary, or it might be permanent. Right now, you know they are not healthy for you. Boundaries are part of love. Letting go can be, too.

Letting go doesn't always require confrontation. If someone is toxic, manipulative, or emotionally abusive, engaging them may only invite drama or gaslighting. If you've set boundaries and been ignored, silence may be your best path forward. With others, mutual respect might allow for a conversation and closure. There may also be a middle ground—gradually lessening your involvement.

You will feel tremendous *relief* when you release unhealthy relationships.

Don't beat yourself up for holding on too long—we all do it. As you release certain people, take a moment to express gratitude. What did they teach you? How did you grow? Many of them were your teachers.

Part of self-love is surrounding yourself with people who accept you as you are—and who love and support you without judgment.

Letting Go — The Soft Power of Surrender

"Letting go isn't a weakness. It's trust. It's choosing peace over control, love over fear, and freedom over attachment. It's the quiet revolution of the soul."
-Lisa Bromfield

Letting go of someone or something that no longer serves you is an act of courage.

What did surrender look like for me?

For most of my adult life, I saw myself as a successful salesperson. I could sell anything—technology, services, ideas. I was persuasive, magnetic, and always prepared. My career wasn't just what I did—it became who I was. My self-worth was wrapped up in my achievements, and I wore my success like armor.

Letting go of that version of myself was one of the most difficult acts of surrender. I had always been an overachiever—pushing hard, striving to prove something. Working in sales magnified that drive. I didn't feel truly accepted unless I was performing at a high level. External validation mattered deeply because it made me feel seen. But the constant pressure to achieve was quietly draining me.

There was pride in my independence. I had nice things, a beautiful home, a loving partner. From the outside, my life looked ideal.

But slowly, something started to unravel.

The work that once energized me began to feel hollow. I no longer wanted to sell. I didn't want to push or convince or prove. It felt like I was playing a role that no longer fit—and the more I tried to hang on, the more disconnected I felt.

At the same time, my relationship ended. Ten years of shared dreams vanished in a moment, and I was left alone in a house that no longer felt like home.

That was when surrender truly began.

I had to surrender the version of myself I had worked so hard to build—the driven, successful, partnered woman. I had to release the identity that had given me safety and recognition. And I had to face the truth: I had no idea who I was without it all.

It was terrifying. But in that space of not knowing, something softer began to emerge.

I didn't jump into another job. I didn't chase a new relationship. I got still. I began to listen. And eventually, I started to follow the gentle tug of my soul—the part of me that longed to heal, to guide, to serve in a different way.

What came forward wasn't flashy or marketable. It wasn't polished. It was real.

I became a Reiki practitioner. A psychic. A channel. A writer. A truth-teller.

And most surprising of all—I discovered I could be *happy* without a partner. I could be whole, right here, right now. No one to impress. Nothing to prove.

Surrendering my identity wasn't a loss. It was a return—to myself.

Letting go of that old identity felt like a rebirth—raw, painful, and filled with fear. I had no idea who I was becoming. I only knew that I had to trust and have faith that it would all work out. I was in the process of recreating myself from a place of knowing "I am enough." I didn't need anyone's approval any more.

When you listen to your inner voice say, "It's time to let go, to release the grip of the things you have been clinging on to, that no longer serve you, and hand it over to your higher power," you will feel a peace inside of you that has eluded you for so long. You are now choosing yourself—above everything and everyone else—honoring your worth in a way you never have before.

Grief and Loss

"Grief is the soil in which our next self takes root. In honoring the pain of what's lost, we cultivate the strength to bloom anew."
— Anonymous

As you shed this old version of yourself, shift your identity, and go through significant life changes, you will let go of the person you once were—the habits, beliefs, and ways of thinking that no longer serve you—in order to make space for a new version of yourself. This process is as real and complex as losing a loved one. You are essentially mourning the person you have outgrown, so there are a few things to keep in mind.

First, acknowledge the end of a chapter in your life, which may involve relationships or a career. Allow yourself to cry and feel the loss. You may feel angry, sad, or confused—or, on the opposite side of the spectrum, excitement and joy. You will indeed be riding an emotional roller coaster.

Be gentle and patient with yourself. There is no rush. Don't compare yourself to others around you. Take time to reflect on your growth, what you have learned, and celebrate this! Embrace exactly where you are in your life, and have gratitude.

Practice self-care daily, committing to yourself emotionally and physically. Meditation, journaling, movement, a massage, a spa day—do what brings you joy! Be deeply compassionate and loving to yourself as you grieve. This is an exhausting and painful part of your journey. It's so uncomfortable that, at times, you will want to go back to your old self because it is easier.

There is no going back—keep telling yourself this.

Take a moment each day and be grateful for that old person you are letting go of and the new one you are becoming.

Energy Work

"The body is a self-healing organism, so it's really about clearing things out of the way so the body can heal itself."
—Barbara Brennan

I believe that receiving energy work is key to your healing journey. Reiki, qigong, acupuncture, Emotional Freedom Technique, Healing Touch, tai chi, Pranic Healing, breathwork, crystal healing, and shamanic healing are just some forms that you can access.

Why is it so important to incorporate energy work during your spiritual awakening and journey? This is because your mind, body, and spirit are going through a major transformation. Energy work clears blockages and balances emotions, allowing your body to vibrate at a higher frequency. As your consciousness expands, energy work supports you through these transitions so that you don't feel drained, helping your body adjust to the higher vibrations.

On a physical level, energy work calms the nervous system, providing more grounding and stability. This helps reduce stress, anxiety, and insomnia. By balancing the body on a physical level, it invites a more harmonious and peaceful state of being. You will feel more grounded and focused and more connected to your authentic self.

Fear is one of the biggest obstacles to your growth. When fear is activated, it triggers a stress response known as 'fight or flight.' This results in many physical consequences, such as increased heart rate and blood pressure, muscle tension, and digestive issues, to name a few. Energy work helps you release fears and resistance so that as you awaken, you will be more open to receiving new relationships, careers, and life purposes. It unlocks a space to attract what is for your highest and best good.

While living in Phoenix, I received many signs that I should train as a Reiki practitioner. The next part of my journey involved delving deeper into energy work. Interestingly, just like my first teacher, I was already incorporating energy work into my private sessions with clients. I had an inner knowing that formal training would take me to the next level.

Sure enough, I met my Reiki Master Teacher in Florida, marking yet another turning point for immense change.

What is Reiki? Reiki is the harnessing of Life Force Energy. The word *Rei* means "Universal," and *Qi* (also spelled *Chi* or *Ki*) means "life force energy." We all have access to it. Qi is the vital energy that flows through all living things, sustaining life, health, and balance. It moves through pathways in the body called meridians—highways where energy circulates and interacts with various organs and systems. Each meridian is associated with a specific organ (such as the lungs, liver, or kidneys) and plays a crucial role in both physical and emotional well-being. When Qi flows smoothly, the body remains healthy and in harmony. However, blockages or imbalances can lead to discomfort or illness.

When your Qi is balanced, you feel energized and healthy on both emotional and physical levels. To maintain this balance, you can receive a Reiki treatment, acupuncture, or practice qigong or tai chi. Meditation is also an invaluable tool.

A Reiki practitioner channels energy from Source, acting as a conduit for healing. We are not healers! Rather, we facilitate the flow of healing energy from a Higher Power to each client.

The focus of Reiki healing is on the chakras—the seven main energy centers in the body through which life force energy flows. While the concept of chakras originated in India and were not part of Reiki's origin in Japan, the two practices complement each other beautifully.

Each chakra corresponds to specific physical, emotional, and spiritual aspects of life. When they are balanced, overall well-being is enhanced. When blocked, they can contribute to physical ailments or emotional struggles.

The **1st Degree of Reiki** focuses on self-healing. Students learn hand placements for self-treatment and embark on a 21-day journey, practicing Reiki on themselves daily for at least 30 minutes. They also explore the history of Reiki and its emotional impact. After this attunement, students are only authorized to practice on themselves—not on others.

The **2nd Degree of Reiki** introduces sacred symbols that allow practitioners to work on others—both in person and remotely—as well as on animals. In my teaching practice, this is followed by Advanced Reiki Training (Reiki Master) and then Reiki Master Teacher training for those who wish to instruct others.

It's important to understand that these levels are not hierarchical. Each level is not "better" than the one before—it simply represents a deeper commitment to the practice and to oneself.

Crystals and Energy Work

Another powerful tool in energy work is crystals. These natural formations serve as amplifiers and transformers of energy, helping to clear blockages and restore balance. Here are a few examples:

- **Clear Quartz** – Known as the "Master Healer," it clears the mind of negativity and enhances spiritual receptivity.
- **Amethyst** – Promotes spiritual growth and emotional balance while providing protection from negative energy.
- **Black Tourmaline** – Creates a powerful energetic shield, grounding and protecting against unwanted influences.

- **Rose Quartz** – Opens the heart chakra, promoting self-love and healing emotional wounds.
- **Selenite** – Clears and charges other crystals while purifying spaces and auras.
- **Citrine** – Attracts abundance and transforms negative energy into positive vibrations.

To work with crystals, start by cleansing them with moonlight or burning sage. Hold them and set clear intentions, allowing their natural frequencies to align with your energy field. You can place them in your space, wear them, or use them during meditation to amplify their benefits.

When visiting a crystal store, trust your intuition. Often, you will be drawn to the crystals you need. A good test is placing a crystal in your left hand (the receiving hand). If your palm warms up, this is a sign that the crystal resonates with you—take it home!

Qigong

Another valuable energy practice is qigong, which involves gentle body tapping to stimulate Qi flow through the meridians. This method blends acupressure with movement, helping to open energy pathways and restore balance.

In Traditional Chinese Medicine, qigong is used to harmonize *Yin* and *Yang*—the essential forces of balance in the body. A great resource is Michael Chang, a qigong practitioner who offers clear instructional videos on YouTube. Even a five-minute Qigong routine can be easily integrated into your daily life.

Energy work has been central to my transformation. My daily commitment to self-healing with Reiki, meditation, and energy balancing has become non-negotiable.

Phyllis Furumoto, the granddaughter of Hawayo Takata (who introduced Reiki to the U.S. in 1937), beautifully captures the essence of energy mastery, *"Mastery is a state of being."*

Once you learn to harness life force energy—whether through Reiki, crystals, qigong, or meditation—you will cultivate an unshakable inner peace. True mastery is not about external control; it's about maintaining tranquility and balance within—no matter what chaos surrounds you.

Theo the "Healer"

My book wouldn't be complete without mentioning my cat, Theo. He's become quite the sensation on social media, always making a cameo during my live streams on TikTok. The audience goes wild when he appears—he's truly a character.

On April 23, 2010, my partner and I decided it was time to welcome another furry friend into our home. I made a trip to the Humane Society in Phoenix and stumbled upon a litter of kittens that had just arrived from foster care.

One tan-colored, eight-week-old male kitten immediately caught my eye. I've always had a soft spot for cats with that coloring. When Laurie and I separated in 2013, all of the cats stayed with me. It wasn't until I became a Reiki practitioner that I realized how deeply Theo is connected to Source. Reiki self-treatment is a non-negotiable and essential part of my daily practice.

Each morning, I find a quiet spot—usually on my bed—to meditate for at least twenty minutes and then give myself Reiki for another thirty minutes. Like clockwork, Theo climbs into my lap every single time. If I delay too long in doing my morning practice, he'll meow and pester me until I finally sit down. He keeps me accountable to my practice. Sophie and Zeke generally join too, peacefully laying next to me.

Let's take a moment to reflect on pets and the sacred role they can play in our spiritual lives.

Animals are incredibly sensitive to energy and emotion. They often detect subtle energetic shifts long before we become consciously aware of them. Cats, in particular, are believed to absorb or transmute negative energy. They bring a steady, soulful, and quiet presence. Dogs, on the other hand, tend to offer grounding energy and a more overt expression of unconditional love.

Our pets often mirror our emotional states, and when we're out of energetic balance, they can sometimes become ill themselves. They are powerful stabilizers during turbulent times—true companions and healers in fur coats. They always seem to arrive in our lives at just the right moment.

Tune into your pets. Notice how they respond to your energy when you're calm—or when you're a hot mess. Let them be part of your spiritual practice. My cats love when I clear the energy in my home using my drum or singing bowls. Theo especially loves Reiki; he soaks up the energy during my self-treatments. But it's not a one-way exchange—I can feel his healing presence flowing back to me.

My cats Sophie, Theo, and Zeke each bring a unique and special presence into my home. They've been my loyal companions through so much.

On the days when I was in tears, feeling lost or broken, they were there—holding space for me in their quiet, unassuming way. They've never judged me. They've simply loved me.

In their own way, they have been some of my greatest teachers—reminding me, again and again, of the power of unconditional love.

Creating a Daily Practice

"Success is the sum of small efforts, repeated day in and day out."
—*Robert Collier*

I invite you to shift your perspective on using spiritual tools. Any new method you explore—whether it's meditation, journaling, breathwork, or energy healing—should be rooted in one thing: loving yourself more deeply.

There is no "perfect" way to meditate or journal. What matters most is that your practice feels nurturing. It's not a task—it's an act of love.

Create a sacred space just for you. Even a small corner of a room can become a sanctuary. Place a small table or shelf there and turn it into a simple altar. Add photos of loved ones, a candle, crystals, or keepsakes from those who've passed. You might play calming music or use a diffuser with lavender essential oil to enhance the energy.

Think of this daily practice as a sacred appointment with your soul. At first, you may resist—silence often brings up emotions we've tucked away. That's okay. Be gentle with yourself. This is your time to heal, to reconnect, to remember who you are.

Let this be something you look forward to. Because showing up for yourself is the most loving thing you can do.

Consistency. Repetition. These are what will get you the best results. Your daily spiritual practice must become non-negotiable—nothing should interfere with it.

The toolkit that I'm offering you in this book is full of practices and methods you can use, but here are a few suggestions I believe will truly set you up for success.

First, use a calendar—whether it's on your phone, a paper planner, or even one stuck on your refrigerator. Write down the specific practices you want to incorporate: meditation, journaling, body movement, and any other tools that resonate with you. Then, assign specific times each day to follow through with these practices.

This simple act of scheduling helps you stay accountable and creates a routine that supports your growth.

Here's an example of what a daily practice might look like:

- **Meditation:** Before getting out of bed, plug into a guided meditation, listen to calming music, or sit in silence. Start with five minutes and gradually extend it, beginning your day in stillness and connection.
- **Journaling:** Perhaps over your morning beverage, open your journal and pour out the thoughts spinning in your head. It's a great way to quiet the "monkey mind" and begin the day with clarity.
- **Gratitude:** In your journal, list at least three things you're grateful for. Gratitude expands everything in your life. This can serve as a reminder to keep noticing and appreciating even the smallest things throughout your day.
- **Affirmations:** Write down your affirmations and say them aloud. Remember, you're reprogramming old limiting beliefs and shifting your internal dialogue.
- **Body Movement:** Move your body with intention. Whether it's a gym session, a gentle walk, yoga, tai chi, or qi gong—just move. Movement helps clear stagnant energy and reconnects you to your body.
- **Nature Time:** Spend time outside. Walk in nature. Breathe. This calms your parasympathetic nervous system and helps you stay grounded and

present.

Let me share a deeper glimpse of my own practice. When I wake up, I begin with at least twenty minutes of meditation, followed by over thirty minutes of Reiki self-treatment. My day includes preparing healthy, nourishing meals, and spending time outside—walking, hiking, or biking. Later in the day, I head to the gym for a 30-minute weight session, followed by ten peaceful minutes on the hydromassage bed.

Now, what if you committed to a daily spiritual practice for the next seven days?

Track how you feel in your journal. Notice what shifts. Don't underestimate the power of your daily devotion—it's not just a habit; it's a spiritual muscle you're building in your journey of loving yourself.

Your commitment to your daily practice is the greatest statement of self-love—to yourself and to the Universe. You will see results. I promise.

Plant Medicine

"The transformative power of plant medicine lies in its ability to dissolve the barriers of the ego and reveal the intricate tapestry of life that connects us all."
-Anonymous

On July 29, 2023, I was attuned as a Reiki Master Teacher. Over the next month, I completely unraveled. This took me down a path I never thought I would explore.

I realized I had been masking depression for many years. My inner wounded child surfaced, and I went down a rabbit hole. My dearest friend in Arizona urged me to see a therapist. I asked my Guides to bring me the right person—and they delivered in a big way.

The therapist was holistic, and immediately recommended that I try a psilocybin journey. I never use drugs or alcohol, so this was uncharted territory for me. I won't deny it—I was scared. But after reading the studies, I knew I had to move forward.

The practitioner came to my home and spent five hours with me. Two days afterward, I felt euphoric. I journaled and walked outside, feeling a renewed sense of clarity. Over the next few months, the depression never returned. Now, two years later, I remain depression-free.

Disclaimer: I am not a physician, nor am I recommending that you stop any medications or take plant medicine. I am simply sharing research on psilocybin so that you can understand its potential benefits.

A study by Johns Hopkins University shows a significant impact of psilocybin on depression. "Psilocybin not only produces significant and immediate effects, but it also has a long duration which suggests that it may be a uniquely useful new treatment for depression," says Roland Griffiths, professor at the Johns Hopkins University School of Medicine, Founding Director of the Center for Psychedelic and Consciousness Research. "Compared to standard antidepressants, which must be taken for long stretches of time, psilocybin has the potential to enduringly relieve the symptoms of depression with one or two treatments."

Some people choose to experience psilocybin through a guided ceremony, while others microdose. It is not legal in all states and countries. If you are interested, finding a spiritual community may connect you with plant medicine practitioners. Some also explore Ayahuasca and even travel to Peru to work with a shaman.

Again, it all comes down to tuning into what you need. Explore different methods and practitioners, and see what resonates with you.

Movement as Medicine

> *"When you put the body in motion, you will find not only health but wholeness."*
> — Donna Farhi

Much of my spiritual awakening included hiking solo all over the U.S. and Canada. These trips were instrumental in connecting more deeply with myself through nature. It was a time to enjoy my own company without a partner so I could learn what my heart and soul truly needed.

Movement doesn't mean you have to be a marathon runner! You can incorporate a simple and short daily workout routine. Energy gets "stuck" and stagnant in our bodies, so even walking just 15 minutes a day will make a difference. My gym workout is no longer than thirty minutes a few times a week. Some days I take short walks, other days I go on longer hikes.

I have some days when I wake up and I can tell I feel "off." A five minute qigong practice always makes me feel better. Sometimes, I'll jump right into a twenty minute yoga practice with Yoga by Adriene on YouTube. She rocks! Or playing a favorite song on Spotify and dancing to it.

Movement is often considered medicine because it helps facilitate healing, integration, and connection with both the body and the self.

Why Movement is So Powerful

As you release old patterns of behavior, emotions and memories will bubble to the surface. Practices like yoga, martial arts, and dance can help clear stagnant energy in the body, allowing for spiritual clearing.

Moving your body is part of grounding and centering. Whether it be walking, stretching, breathwork, or weight workouts, it will help you feel more connected to yourself and more present in the moment.

Unprocessed feelings and traumas reside in the body. Any type of movement can assist in healing you at a cellular level, releasing emotional and physical blockages.

If you are tapping into your authentic self, movement can facilitate your transformation. Each movement, step, or stretch reflects growth, change, and expansion in both the physical and spiritual realms.

Conscious movement shifts energy through posture, breath, and motion, interrupting negative thought patterns. This creates momentum for positive change. The key is choosing activities that energize rather than deplete you.

Select movement that brings joy and can become a natural part of your daily rhythm. Even simple dance breaks elevate vibration and mood. We are beings of energy, frequency, and vibration.

When we raise our personal energy through movement, we not only help ourselves, we help the collective energy. We are all interconnected—as human beings, plants, animals, the environment, and even on an unseen level. The change inside us is felt all over the planet!

As you move through your spiritual awakening, remember—it's a balance of the mind, body, and spirit. You are developing more awareness and tuning into your body's needs.

Your body is your partner in transformation. Honor it with a movement that feels like a celebration rather than an obligation.

Nature

"In every walk with nature one receives far more than he seeks."
— John Muir

In combination with meditation, energy work, and working with various mentors, one essential ingredient in your journey of "becoming" this new version of yourself is spending time outside in nature.

My solo hiking trips became invitations to turn more deeply inside of me, where I knew I would find the answers. There were no distractions—I was miles away from any outside noise. In Glacier National Park, I hiked over fifty-five miles, immersed in the sounds of the wind through the trees and the vastness of the sky above me. In the early morning, as the sun rose, I drove silently along the winding park roads, stopping to view the magnificent glaciers covered in snow. I often saw bears accompanied by their cubs, and I was in complete awe of the beauty around me. After hiking for several hours, I watched the sun set over the glaciers and embraced deep gratitude for the day.

In 2019, I revisited Banff, Canada, a place I had hiked on my 50th birthday seven years earlier. The Canadian Rockies, with their towering peaks and dramatic landscapes, are unlike anything you can find in the United States. As I drove down the Trans-Canada Highway, the sheer size of the mountains took my breath away.

When I arrived at the trail near Chateau Lake Louise, I stared at the balcony outside one of the rooms. My ex had treated me to a stay in the Glacier Suite, and I remembered standing on that balcony, looking over Lake Louise. It was a healing moment, intertwined with sadness and joy. I secured my backpack, pulled out my hiking poles, and began my hike.

At the beginning of the trail, I ran into a husband and wife from Germany. The husband said, "Aren't you afraid of hiking this trail because of the bears?"

I replied, "Nope! Follow me! Let's make a day of this."

We spent the day together, hiking over 14 miles, with the wife assuming the role of navigator. Along the way, we met some other people from Germany, and the four of them chatted away in their native language. We were determined to visit both tea houses that were built along the trail, despite the snow that had fallen the evening before. The Lake Agnes Tea House opened in 1904; the Plain of Six Glaciers Tea House in the 1920's. It was common practice to stop and have a snack and tea at each of these houses.

The scenery touched every part of my heart and soul—the sun sparkling off the snow, the trickling of streams, the cool mountain air—a feeling that, to this day, I have not experienced in any other park. By the end of the day, we celebrated our feat, joyful over our shared experiences.

Nature is where I connect more deeply to myself and to the divine. It keeps me grounded and present, allowing me to focus on the sights, sounds, and natural rhythms around me. It removes all of life's daily distractions, providing a way to focus on doing the "inside" work. Spending time in nature has helped me cultivate a deeper sense of humility, compassion, and understanding that we are all connected as one.

There are many ways to connect with nature! Go for a swim, watch the sunrise or sunset, or do some gardening. You can meditate, journal, or even practice yoga or tai chi outside. Try sitting on the ground, leaning against a tree, or even hugging it! Tree energy is incredibly powerful.

Trees help create a stabilizing force, as their roots are deeply anchored into the earth. By connecting with them, you'll absorb their energy and feel more grounded, centered, and present. The tree acts as your ally, absorbing any negative or heavy energy and restoring balance. Its energy harmonizes your state of being, bringing you peace even amidst chaos.

After connecting with nature—the trees, the wind, the sun, and the clouds—take a moment to express your gratitude. Place your hand on the tree's trunk to exchange energy, and speak words of thanks aloud to the natural world around you.

Grounding and Centering

"When you are grounded in the present moment, your energy is peaceful, and you are at home with yourself."
– Thich Nhat Hanh

There are times when you may feel disconnected, anxious, overwhelmed, stressed, or emotionally turbulent. This is when a grounding practice will help reel you in and re-center your energy. When I feel this way, I step into my backyard, place my bare feet on the earth, and take a few deep, steady breaths. I listen to the sounds around me—birds singing, wind in the trees—and allow myself to simply be. I take a moment to express gratitude for another day and anchor myself in the present moment. This simple practice grounds my energy and reminds me that peace is always within reach.

What is grounding?

It's a practice of anchoring your energy into the present moment, creating more stability and balance.

Grounding can be done by placing your bare feet on the earth. This is more commonly known as 'earthing,' a powerful technique that involves connecting your bare feet to grass, soil, or sand. It has been shown to reduce inflammation, improve sleep, reduce stress and anxiety, boost immune function, and reduce pain, to mention a few. I recommend watching *The Earthing Movie* (2019) on YouTube to understand the potential benefits further. You can also purchase a grounding mat to do this indoors, as well as grounding sheets.

Spending time in nature has been shown to reduce symptoms of depression, anxiety, and mood disorders. It enhances both your physical and mental well-being, fosters gratitude, and helps you feel more connected to yourself.

Engage your senses fully—listen to the sounds around you, feel the breeze on your skin, and watch leaves dance in the wind. These simple acts activate your body's natural relaxation response. Whether walking forest paths, tending gardens, or simply sitting beneath the open sky, nature restores our essential balance.

You may have also heard of the Japanese concept of *Forest Bathing*, known in Japan as *Shinrin-yoku*, which reinforces these healing benefits. This practice of immersing yourself in a forest environment has been widely recognized for its physical, mental, and emotional benefits.

Spiritual Hygiene and Protection

*"The degree to which you maintain your own energy field will
determine the quality of your life."*
— *Barbara Brennan*

Previously, I discussed that we are made up of energy, which vibrates at different frequencies, and influences our thoughts, emotions, and physical well-being. Just as you take care of your body through regular hygiene practices, the same applies to your energy field.

What is an energy field? It is an invisible, yet tangible, field of energy that surrounds every living thing, including humans, animals, and even objects. It's often referred to as the aura in spiritual or holistic practices. This energy field is thought to be a reflection of our physical, emotional, mental, and spiritual states.

Cleansing your energy field keeps it free of stagnant, negative energy. It keeps your energy flowing fluidly, preventing blockages. It also helps with your physical and emotional health.

Why is it important to cleanse your home and your physical energy?

We each have a unique energy field, that when exposed to stress and other environmental factors, creates imbalances. This shows up as anxiety, depression, fatigue, and illness. You can also feel heavy, uncomfortable and drained when your energy field becomes clogged, so to speak. Our energy and the energy in our home can become stagnant. So pay attention and tune into how you feel each day. Cleansing your energy field and your home is just like taking a cozy, warm shower.

Some of the benefits of cleansing your physical body are enhancing your well-being. You will feel lifted and more positive. You will actually notice a calm and balanced feeling, and this will raise your vibration and frequency so that you can move with more ease throughout the day.

The simplest technique to cleanse your body and home involves these methods:

- **Smudging-** This can be done by burning sage or palo santo.
- **Sound-** Using tingsha bells, a singing bowl, or a drum.
- **Clearing Spray-** Filling a glass spray bottle with distilled water and sage essential oil.

(Please use caution when burning sage, palo santo, or using essential oils around pets. Many essential oils and plant-based smudging products can be toxic to animals, particularly cats, dogs, and birds.)

Let me share how I practice cleansing and protection:

1. First, I cleanse my body using a sage spray.
2. I call in Michael the Archangel. He is not a religious figure. He is associated with cleansing and purification. He is also a source of protection. I utilize one of the tools listed in number one; I call him in to clear my body of anything negative or heavy.
3. Once I have cleansed my body, I cleanse my house at least once a week. This is done by accessing a home cleansing prayer, and saying it at your front door. Then, I move in a clockwise manner throughout my home with my cleansing tool, going into closets and cabinets, finishing at the front door in gratitude.
4. For protection, I simply call in Michael each day after I meditate.

You can access some wonderful cleansing prayers on the internet. Here is an example of one:

"*Divine Light,*
I call upon your presence now.
Surround me and this space with your pure, healing energy.
Cleanse my body of all that no longer serves me—
release tension, fear, and anything I've absorbed that is not mine.
Restore me to balance, wholeness, and peace.
I ask that this home be cleared of any lingering heaviness or unwanted energy.
Fill every room, every corner, with light, love, and protection.
Let this space be a sanctuary of peace, comfort, and joy.
I give thanks for the healing that flows now,
and for the divine presence that blesses this space and my being.
And so it is."

When done regularly, you will notice that you feel better. You can cleanse your body and home as frequently as you like. As you become more in touch with your energy, you will recognize when things feel "off."

With cleansing and protection, find what resonates with you. It's a wonderful ritual and an essential part of self-care and self-love for your emotional and physical well-being.

Sound Healing

"Sound is the medicine of the future."
— *Edgar Cayce*

Sound healing helps harmonize the body—it restores balance in the mind, body, and spirit. As we are energetic beings, frequency and vibration influence us deeply at the cellular level, also impacting our nervous system.

Let me first discuss three of the most important brain wave states—alpha, delta, and theta. These are associated with subconscious healing and create a deep sense of relaxation.

Alpha brain waves occur in everyday life when you are feeling calm, focused, and relaxed. This state is often referred to as the "flow state." You enter this state during meditation, hypnosis, and daydreaming. It allows you to absorb new information and improves your intuition. Sound healing in this state shifts you from a stressful state to a more balanced state.

Theta brain waves facilitate healing at the subconscious level. Just before you fall asleep or as you are waking up, you are in the theta state. This is where you can release deep trauma, self-limiting beliefs, and repressed memories. It is also a powerful state for manifesting your desires. Visualizing something you want to create in your life just before falling asleep allows it to "brew" in your subconscious while you sleep. Sound healing in this state can help release trauma and foster a more peaceful inner state.

Lastly, delta brain waves are the slowest brain waves and affect you at the cellular level, helping to repair the immune system. People who enter a deep state of meditation often report shifting into a state of bliss. Another benefit of sound healing is that it can literally recalibrate the nervous system and induce rest.

So, how can you unlock these different states? You can attend a drumming circle, a gong meditation, or a sound healing session with crystal bowls or Tibetan singing bowls. Participants are immersed in these sounds, which may provide benefits such as deep relaxation, reduced anxiety and stress, emotional release, enhanced mental clarity, energetic balance, and improved sleep.

Lastly, chanting is another powerful modality for healing. It is a great way to quiet the mental chatter in your head. Some people who have difficulty meditating prefer to chant instead.

Chanting stimulates the vagus nerve, which, in turn, activates the parasympathetic nervous system, inducing a restful state. There are different mantras you can use for chanting. Chanting mantras elevates your consciousness, releases negativity, and shifts your energy field. By repeating a mantra, you facilitate the rewiring of your thought patterns.

The most powerful and well-known mantra is chanting, "Om" (AUM). This is believed to represent universal energy. It stimulates the Third Eye (pineal gland), which is connected to higher consciousness and intuition. It balances all the chakras, creating more harmony in the body. It also lowers cortisol levels, allowing you to relax.

Sound healing is a modality of energy healing that is near and dear to my heart. Those of you who have worked privately with me know that I use my Shamanic Drum, "Serena," in each session, along with my Tibetan singing bowls. While most of my clients have never been exposed to a drum before, they all report a deeper feeling of calm and inner peace after the session. And mind you, this is done virtually!

Another option is to invest in a sound healing instrument like a drum, a

Tibetan singing bowl, or a crystal bowl to create your own sound bath. These can be used during meditation or to clear your energy and the energy in your space.

When it comes to drums, you can choose one made from elk, buffalo, or deer skin. For a deeper connection, consider taking a drum-building class, where you can infuse your own energy into the creation of your drum. There's something uniquely special about crafting your own drum, and the resonance of a natural skin drum is unmatched by synthetic materials. However, keep in mind that skin drums are affected by humidity and may need to be tightened with a hair dryer—a minor inconvenience for the powerful experience they offer.

If you're looking for a synthetic option, Remo makes exceptional drums. I personally own their Bahia Buffalo drum. These are not affected by the weather and tend to be more durable than skin-made drums.

If you're new to sound healing instruments, visit a local store that specializes in them so you can try out different instruments and experience their vibrations firsthand. For example, Skinny Beats in Asheville offers an impressive variety, allowing you to find what resonates most with your body.

As you progress through your transformation, the sound healing instruments you use will evolve as well. This is because your vibration and frequency are rising. It's important to take the time to truly feel into each instrument. When you enter a store, it can feel overwhelming—almost like a candy store—there's so much to choose from! But trust your intuition to guide you toward what resonates with you.

You do not have to be musically talented to play any of these instruments. Whether you use them personally or in a group setting, simply enjoy the experience.

A Brief Guide For Your Own Self-Healing Sound Bath

How long should each of your self-healing sound baths be? Here is a short guide:

- 3–5 minutes: Ideal for grounding, energy clearing, or stress relief. You

might do this before meditating, going to sleep, or starting your day.
- 10–15 minutes: Allows you to enter a deeper state of relaxation, shifting your brainwaves into the alpha or theta state.
- 20–30 minutes: Used for full energetic cleansing and chakra balancing.

How do you know when to stop?

Simply listen to your body. If you feel relaxed and at ease, then you have done enough. On the other hand, if you feel overstimulated or restless, this too is a sign that it's time to stop.

In the next section, I will expand on one of the most common obstacles you may face and provide solutions.

Fear

"He who overcomes his fears will truly be free."
—Aristotle

Are you having trouble making decisions because you're afraid of making the wrong one? At the same time, do you feel—deep in your heart and your gut—that you need to take action, only for doubt to creep in again?

Fear is the obstacle that stops you dead in your tracks. It holds you back from your dreams, convincing you that you're not capable or worthy of achieving them.

So, what is fear? It's perfectly captured in this acronym: False Evidence Appearing Real.

Fear creates expectations that are simply not true. It magnifies the "what ifs," projecting the worst possible outcomes.

Fear will always try to derail you. It feeds doubt and urges you to give up. There will be moments when you want to throw in the towel. Fear thrives in your comfort zone and wants to keep you there. One of the greatest fears we face is uncertainty about the future—a fear that often creates anxiety rooted in the feeling of losing control.

There's no shortcut through this. You must be willing to let go of control and allow yourself to surrender. Surrendering often feels scary and uncomfortable—but that space is exactly where true growth can happen.

Let's take a moment to examine your fears with a gentle but powerful exercise. Find a quiet space where you can be undisturbed.

Fear Release Exercise - Identify and Let Go

1. Identify Your Fears

What fears are holding you back?

(Examples: fear of being alone, fear of failure, fear of poverty, fear of judgment, etc.)

2. Feel the Fear

Close your eyes and place your left hand over your heart.

Now say out loud:

"I see you, fear. I'm not going to push you away. Instead, I choose to acknowledge you."

Now, sit with each fear. Notice where it shows up in your body. Be the witness. Just observe—without judgment.

3. Let Go of the Fear

Now say:

"I release this fear. I no longer need you to feel safe. I trust myself and the process."

Visualize a beautiful white-gold light forming a bubble around each fear. See it being transmuted into love and carried into the light.

4. Anchor in Love

Create your own affirmations, or use these examples:

- "I am deeply supported by the Universe."
- "It is safe for me to trust the unfolding of my path."
- "Love is who I am. I return to that knowing now."

Fear Release Exercise - Going Deeper

This next exercise may be painful—but it's powerful. This is where you truly confront your fears.

Close your eyes. Imagine not changing anything—staying exactly where you are—for the next five or ten years.

Feel that deeply.

Let any emotions arise. You may even feel tears welling up.

Sit with this for a few minutes.

Now open your journal and write this question:

What are your fears costing you?

Are they costing you joy? Inner peace? Love? Freedom?

Once you recognize the cost, something shifts. A fire ignites in your heart—and nothing will be able to stop you. You will be invincible!

Solitude

"The quieter you become, the more you can hear."
—Ram Dass

As you progress on your healing journey, your energy will begin to transform. Naturally, this means the energy around you will change as well. The people you spend time with may no longer be the same, and you may find yourself spending more time alone. Don't resist this. You haven't done anything "wrong"—you are evolving!

It's uncomfortable, isn't it? It's supposed to be.

Why are so many people fearful of solitude? Keeping yourself busy is a distraction technique—a way to avoid facing yourself and your feelings.

It may be painful to be by yourself. Emotions you have been burying will come to the surface. In solitude, you will release past pain and integrate changes. It's important to do this without being influenced by the energy of others.

You will tune into your inner voice, gain a deeper understanding of your true self, and become keenly aware of your own needs. Learning to enjoy your own company means doing things by yourself. You will make yourself a priority—this is not selfish! You will begin to believe in yourself like never before, instilling a new confidence, trusting your intuition and gut feelings.

Additionally, you will cultivate a deeper sense of inner peace. This time alone will teach you independence and detachment from external validation. You will align with your soul's purpose, reflecting a more authentic part of yourself.

Know that this solitary period is temporary. Balance is key. At some point, you will be ready to start reconnecting with a new tribe.

So where is a good place to start? Solo date nights! Go to one restaurant once a week by yourself. Sit at the bar where you may interact with another customer. Another activity is to take a day trip somewhere close to home.

Solitude has become my best friend. When I need to recharge, or rethink a situation, it provides a nurturing space for me to connect more deeply with myself and Spirit. Solitude has provided me with a place to retreat. I always come out more refreshed, and with more clarity.

Let solitude be one of your guides to creating a new you.

Journaling: Feel It to Heal It

> *"Writing is medicine. It is an appropriate antidote to injury. It is an appropriate companion for any difficult change."*
> —Julia Cameron

As you experience spending more time with yourself, journaling can become a powerful tool to work through your emotions and feelings. It's cathartic and provides clarity.

The emotions you experience may include anxiety, depression, sadness, and happiness. It's a roller coaster at times—trust me, I know! This is where you use your inner power to accept and acknowledge who you are and where you are in your life. Processing these emotions is part of the healing process—no more ignoring them! Journaling opens a pathway to deeper self-understanding and transformation.

You might be wondering, what should I write in my journal, and how much should I write? Let's walk through this together.

First, buy yourself a special journal—one that feels good.

Now, you are ready!

- Begin each writing session with an **unfiltered release**. Let your thoughts flow without judgment, allowing buried emotions and negative self-talk to surface. This creates space for clarity and healing. Journaling doesn't mean writing page upon page. Some days, you will write a few sentences. Other days, it just keeps flowing! Don't worry about correct grammar or punctuation—just spew out what's on your mind. Get it all down, then reflect on it. Likely, you will gain some clarity.

- Follow your unfiltered release of your feelings with **positive affirmations** that resonate with your spirit. Speak them aloud to amplify their power. These words reshape your inner dialogue, gradually replacing old thought patterns with empowering beliefs.
- **Express gratitude** next, acknowledging at least three blessings. Gratitude is a powerful attractor, drawing more abundance into every area of life. Even if you are struggling, express gratitude! There is a lesson here that you will see more clearly as you write.
- Close by **setting clear intentions**. Write your desires and goals with precision, knowing that putting pen to paper begins their manifestation. Your journal becomes a sacred space where transformation takes root and flourishes. Write it to invite it!

Through consistent practice, journaling becomes your best friend—it documents your journey. Remember, it's progress, not perfection.

At this point in your journey, you may want to explore Julia Cameron's book *The Artist's Way*. I suggest you find a Zoom group to work through this 12-week course. It is truly transformational!

When the book was first published in 1992, it was designed to help individuals overcome creative blocks and unlock their artistic potential. More than just a book, it's a comprehensive 12-week program that guides readers through a spiritual and creative recovery process.

The core premise of the book is that creativity is a spiritual practice that can be nurtured and developed through intentional techniques and mindful approaches. Cameron argues that everyone has creative potential, regardless of their current artistic experience or perceived talents.

Key Components of the Artist's Way Method:

- **Morning Pages:** A daily practice of writing three pages of longhand, stream-of-consciousness writing immediately upon waking. This exercise is designed to clear mental clutter, process emotions, and unblock creative energy.
- **Artist Date:** A weekly solo expedition to nurture the inner creative child. This is a scheduled time for personal exploration and inspiration, such as visiting a museum, taking a nature walk, or engaging in a playful activity that sparks joy and creativity.
- **Spiritual Recovery:** Cameron emphasizes healing the relationship with creativity by addressing inner critical voices, past wounds, and self-limiting beliefs that hinder artistic expression.

When I took this class, I had no expectations. The teacher asked us to start a creative activity, and I had absolutely no clue what that meant for me. I am already quite talented with music, but I wanted something new. So I asked my Guides, and they kept showing me yarn. My mother had tried to teach me how to knit, and I was terrible at it. But for some reason, I kept getting pulled towards a project with yarn.

So off to Joanne Fabric's craft store I went, exploring any aisles associated with yarn. I saw one of those silly machines that you turn with a crank to make hats, but I thought it would be too noisy. Then I saw a crochet hooks. This resonated.

Over the next week, I explored using different sized crochet hooks, and learned that the larger the needle, the easier it was to work with. I began crocheting scarfs, and not only learned that I was good at it, but that it was meditative and calming. Over the next few months, I made a beautiful throw blanket, fingerless gloves, and matching earflap hats for me and my twin.

A creative activity will open up a new channel inside of you, and you will be surprised, like I was, that a talent will show up that you never expected! This beautiful flow of energy will enhance other areas of your life. Creativity is not just an outlet—it's part of your awakening.

What You Resist, Persists

"When you think you've surrendered, surrender more."
—Gabrielle Bernstein

When you fight against something, you inadvertently strengthen the hold of a situation, reality, or emotion. This resistance closes the door for you to receive.

For years, I resisted leaving my sales job. Fear kept me there, as I knew I needed the money to pay my mortgage. All the "what ifs" in my mind had me worrying. When the job ended unexpectedly, something beautiful happened.

It opened up a space for me to receive what I truly deserved—and more! Since then, the Universe has not only provided financial abundance but also with purpose. And for the first time in many years, I was happy—in my heart and in my soul.

Think of resistance as quicksand. The more you thrash, the deeper you sink. But when you relax and spread your weight, you find stability. This applies to all of life's challenges—from difficult emotions to unwanted circumstances.

Notice what you are resisting. Ask yourself, *"Why am I resisting this change? What is my deepest fear?"*

Once you have this inner conversation, you will find the key to unlocking the door of resistance. You will release the struggle, the resistance, and move into a space of surrender. It means aligning with your higher wisdom and allowing things to unfold naturally.

Surrender is not about giving up—it's about releasing control and trusting in the flow of life. It's about loosening your grip on the steering wheel and moving to the passenger seat, allowing a greater force to guide you.

When you finally surrender, you allow the Universe to work its magic. "Allowing" is an act of trust and faith. This is when you stop grasping for what you want and start allowing life to unfold. Synchronicities and signs from the Universe will guide your way.

Trust in divine timing. The Universe operates on its own timing, which likely will not match your need for immediate results. There will be delays and detours along the way, which teach trust, faith, and patience.

When I transitioned from a 30-year career in sales to embracing my abilities as an energy healer and psychic, I had to let go of the identity I had spent my life building. It was one of the hardest things I've ever done. But in surrendering that old identity, I created an entirely new version of myself.

When life feels like it's falling apart, it's actually falling together. On the most difficult days, Spirit encouraged me to pause, rest, and nurture myself. Those moments of stillness allowed me to reset so I could return with more focus and commitment.

Be willing to reinvent yourself. The analogy of a caterpillar turning into a butterfly is fitting. You will morph, transform, and evolve into someone you will not recognize.

How Do You Surrender?

Here are a few exercises you can try.

Create Presence with Mindfulness by Tuning into Your Senses

- **5** things you can see
- **4** things you can feel
- **3** things you can hear
- **2** things you can smell

- **1** thing you can taste

This helps you focus and ground your energy. It shifts your attention away from pain. Getting outside and connecting with nature is especially effective.

Radical Acceptance

Choose a situation in your life where you feel resistance or frustration. It could be something small, like an unexpected change in your routine, or something larger, like a relationship issue.

Instead of resisting, allow yourself to fully feel whatever emotions come up. Accept that things are as they are right now.

Say to yourself, *"I accept things as they are, and I trust that the Universe has a plan for me."* Feel the weight of resistance start to lift as you let go of the need to control the outcome.

A Surrender Prayer

Sit quietly, with your hands open in your lap or raised to the sky, in a posture of receptivity.

Close your eyes and speak a prayer or affirmation such as, *"I surrender my desires to the Universe. I trust that whatever is meant for me will come in its perfect time."*

If you prefer, visualize releasing a balloon with all your worries, desires, or the need for control attached to it. Watch it float away, feeling lighter as it disappears into the sky.

The Negativity Bias

"All that we are is the result of what we have thought. The mind is everything. What we think, we become."
— The Dhammapada

So now you say, *"Lisa, nothing is going right for me. Why is it so difficult to make changes in the direction of my life?"*

The negativity bias refers to the psychological phenomenon where we tend to give more weight to negative experiences, emotions, or information than to positive or neutral ones. This bias can influence decision-making, memory, perception, and behavior, often leading people to focus more on potential threats or risks than on opportunities or positive outcomes.

The negativity bias likely evolved as a survival mechanism. Early humans who were more attuned to threats (e.g., predators, dangerous environments) were better equipped to survive and pass on their genes. As a result, our brains are wired to prioritize negative information as a way to protect ourselves.

Let me give you some examples. News stories on television often focus on negative events, as they receive more attention than positive stories. Criticism in a relationship, work, or from a family member often outweighs any positive feedback.

Dr. Rick Hanson, a neurologist, shares that "the brain is like Teflon to positive experiences, and Velcro to negative experiences. It takes at least five positive experiences to undo a negative experience."

This is where neuroplasticity comes in—the brain's amazing ability to adapt, reorganize, and rewire itself over time. Even as adults, our brains are not fixed. Through repeated focus on positive thoughts, feelings, and experiences, we can actually train our brains to become more resilient, calm, and joyful. The more we practice this, the stronger those new neural pathways become—just like building a muscle.

Now think about the narrative in your head each day—the story you live in that tells you that you are not enough, that you are not deserving or worthy, or that you are never going to be abundant. How do you change the course of this titanic in your head? Let's discuss this further.

What Are Beliefs?

"Beliefs have the power to create and the power to destroy."
—*Tony Robbins*

Beliefs are deeply held convictions or ideas that we accept as true. They shape how we perceive the world, ourselves, and others. They can be either conscious or subconscious. Either way, they play a crucial role in creating our reality. Beliefs are decisions you have made based on experiences and conditioning.

For much of my life, I believed I wasn't enough. I constantly tried to prove myself to others—especially my mother. Her criticism planted a false belief deep within me, one that seeped into everything I was creating: relationships, jobs, and situations. I kept attracting romantic partners that would cheat on me. I worked in pharmaceutical sales where the managers were demeaning and cruel.

The good news is this: We have the power to change our beliefs.

Are your current beliefs empowering or are they self-limiting?

Replace limiting beliefs with ones that align with your goals and values. Reinforce them through repetition and action.

One of the greatest beliefs ingrained in us is that we are "not enough." This makes us feel unworthy and undeserving. So many of us believe we are not enough because of our past, our mistakes, and how people have hurt us.

The truth is this: You are whole, even in your pain. The key is learning to love yourself—not just when you are at your best, but also when you are struggling.

The belief and feeling that *"I am not enough"* holds profound power, both psychologically and emotionally. This belief can have a massive impact on your life, creating a self-fulfilling prophecy. When we feel inadequate, we project that energy outward, attracting situations and relationships that reinforce our perceived unworthiness.

We might self-sabotage through procrastination, avoid making decisions, or settle for less than we deserve—all behaviors that stem from this fundamental belief.

The three words *"I am enough"* challenges negative beliefs, creating space for healing and self-compassion. You become more self-accepting, fostering emotional resilience and a healthier self-image.

This shift in belief can ripple through every aspect of your life. Relationships become healthier as you attract people who reflect your self-worth. Career opportunities expand as you step into your power. Abundance flows more freely as you recognize your deservingness.

The mere fact that you exist is enough. You are and always have been enough. You do not have to do anything or be anything to be loved and accepted. It is the unconditional love you have for yourself—met with compassion and understanding despite your flaws and imperfections—that truly matters.

Our sense of unworthiness deeply impacts our actions, often leading us to become people-pleasers. No one takes your power away; you freely give it away every time you try to prove yourself to gain acceptance or earn love.

To compound matters further, you apologize for the smallest things when no apology is necessary. You continue to drain your own power when you say "yes" when you mean "no." This is a deeply ingrained behavior, and breaking this pattern is not easy. You do not have to compromise your values to be loved. Once you believe in your worthiness and set healthy boundaries, the need to please everyone will no longer be necessary.

Releasing the need for external approval empowers you to recognize that your worth is not dependent upon others' opinions. You will stop comparing your journey to everyone else's, understanding that we each forge a unique path. This realization is liberating and unleashes a new power within you.

This is where you reclaim your power and live authentically. You cultivate a deeper sense of self-worth and confidence, allowing you to move forward with greater certainty.

A book worthy of mention is *The Four Agreements* by Don Miguel Ruiz, one that I read at the beginning of my awakening. It serves as a reminder that personal freedom and happiness come from breaking self-limiting beliefs.

You will learn to adopt new agreements that align with truth and love. He presents four guiding principles:

- **Be Impeccable with Your Word** – Always speak with integrity and use your words for truth and love rather than negativity.
- **Don't Take Anything Personally** – People's actions, opinions, and words are a reflection of their emotions, beliefs, and experiences. It is not about you; it is about something they have not healed. Their behavior is about them, not you!
- **Don't Make Assumptions** – Never assume what someone is thinking or feeling! This will lead you down a rabbit hole. Misunderstandings arise from making assumptions. Instead, ask clarifying questions.
- **Always Do Your Best** – Release any judgment of yourself. Every day, do the best you can. Let go of regrets and the idea that you are making mistakes. Remember, you are learning from each experience!

Keep in mind. You are not broken. You do not need fixing. You need more loving.
Let's do an exercise: audit your self-limiting beliefs.
Grab a piece of paper and divide it into four sections.

1. **In the left column**, identify your self-limiting beliefs. They might include things like *"I am not enough"* or *"I will never succeed."*
2. **In the next column**, write down where you think this belief came from

(childhood, past failures, a bad relationship, etc.).
3. **Now, carefully review what you have written.** Challenge the validity of each statement. Are they true?
4. **In the fourth column, reframe them.** Take each limiting belief and rewrite it in an empowering way.

Here are some examples:

- Self-Limiting Belief: "I'm not good enough."

Empowering Belief: *"I am whole and worthy exactly as I am. Every day I grow into more of my potential."*

- Self-Limiting Belief: "I don't deserve love."

Empowering Belief: *"I am inherently lovable and attract love by being my authentic self."*

- Self-Limiting Belief: "It's too late for me."

Empowering Belief: *"It's never too late to begin. My timing is divine and perfect for my journey."*

- Self-Limiting Belief: "I always fail."

Empowering Belief: *"Every setback is a setup for growth and deeper wisdom."*

- Self-Limiting Belief: "I need to be perfect to be accepted."

Empowering Belief: *"My imperfections make me real, relatable, and beautifully human."*

- Self-Limiting Belief: "Money is hard to come by."

Empowering Belief: *"Money flows to me with ease when I am aligned with my purpose and value."*

- Self-Limiting Belief: "I can't trust people."

Empowering Belief: *"I choose to attract and build relationships rooted in trust and mutual respect."*

- "I'm too old to start something new."

Empowering Belief: *"My age is my strength—my life experience is rich and valuable."*

- "I have to do it all alone."

Empowering Belief: *"Support is all around me. I am open to receiving help and guidance."*

- "I'm not smart/talented/creative enough."

Empowering Belief: *"I have unique gifts that are unfolding and expanding each day."*

So, examine your self-limiting beliefs. Why are you holding on to them? *Are your limiting beliefs costing you your happiness?* Your belief system is ultimately the *magnet* that attracts everything in your life.

So, how do you heal "I am not enough"?

The Law of Attraction

"You don't attract what you want. You attract what you are."
—Wayne Dyer

What you put out, you get back. It's as simple as that. The movie *The Secret* (2006) put the law of attraction into mainstream awareness as a powerful tool of creation.

We shape our reality. Think of yourself as a communication tower. Your thoughts, words, and feelings emit energy that will attract corresponding experiences. Where focus goes, energy flows. Choose your thoughts and words with intention.

Hold yourself accountable at the highest level, knowing you are the creator of everything in your life. You created exactly where you are right here, right now.

Everything in the universe is made up of energy, including our thoughts and words. Each of these carries a vibrational frequency, and that frequency can have a profound effect on our lives and the world around us.

Our emotions directly influence our vibrational frequency, which can shift up or down based on our thoughts and feelings. High-frequency states include enlightenment, peace, joy, love, and gratitude. These emotions uplift us, energize our spirit, and align us with positivity. Positive words and thoughts fuel your growth and attract opportunities.

Low-frequency states include fear, grief, apathy, shame, guilt, and anger. These emotions can weigh us down, creating resistance and stagnation in our lives. Negative words and thoughts drain your energy and reinforce limiting beliefs.

Your words and thoughts are tools of creation. They carry energy that can either empower or diminish you. What we think and say shapes our actions, which in turn shape our environment and relationships. Repeated affirmations or self-talk, whether positive or negative, influence beliefs and self-perception.

Imagine that your body is made up of all of these tiny particles that I will refer to as magnets. You either magnetize abundance or something you do not desire. Be mindful of what you say and think. Your words and thoughts act like magnets, pulling experiences into your reality that match their vibration.

You get to choose how you direct your thoughts. This is one thing you can control! These shape how you will experience each moment and each day!

Let me give you an example:

You think and say, "I am never going to be successful." The Universe takes this energy from you and reflects it back to you. You have just created exactly what you do not want. I like to use the analogy of hitting a tennis ball (or maybe I should say pickleball!) against a backboard. The energy you put out is what returns to you.

Let me give you another example using the vibration of gratitude. Gratitude expands everything into abundance. Every morning, part of my meditation practice includes focusing on gratitude. I continue to express gratitude throughout the day, actually verbalizing it to give it a stronger vibration. When I go to bed at night, I again take a moment to be grateful for what I experienced that day.

The key point with creating a gratitude practice is to focus on what you have, not to focus on what is missing. Gratitude shifts your perspective, reframes the situation, and redirects your focus on what you learned.

Everything happens *for* you. If you get into victim energy of something happening *to* you, you will continue to attract things that do not serve you.

During difficult times, it is critical to express gratitude. Initially, this will feel uncomfortable and counterintuitive. Your voice in your head will be saying, *"How can I be grateful for something awful in my life?"*

So, let's get into some ways to shift your vibration and frequency. This is where you start to do the "inside" work. This is where you will unravel and release the fear, the doubts, and the worthiness issues.

Thoughts and Words Create Your Reality

> *"You create your thoughts, your thoughts create your intentions, and your intentions create your reality."*
> — Wayne Dyer

Louise Hay's book *You Can Heal Your Life* revolutionized our understanding of self-talk and its impact on our reality. She illuminated how the constant negative chatter—I call it the "shitty committee" in our heads—shapes our experiences and limits our potential. The key lies in consciously transforming these internal dialogues.

Every thought and word carries creative power. By shifting from self-criticism to self-love through positive affirmations, we begin undoing years of limiting beliefs. This isn't mere positive thinking—it's a profound rewiring of our relationship with ourselves. As we speak to ourselves with greater kindness, our entire reality shifts to match this new vibration.

Louise had her own battle with cervical cancer, and over a number of months, she was able to heal this through intensive mental, emotional, and physical work. She emphasizes that the key to her healing was releasing deeply rooted anger, resentment, and past trauma through forgiveness and affirmations. Additionally, she adopted a holistic approach that included nutritional changes, visualization, and meditation.

She popularized the perspective that disease is "dis-ease" in the body. This suggests that physical illnesses often originate from emotional, mental, or spiritual imbalances.

The process of healing begins with awareness. Notice when you speak unkindly to yourself. Replace "I am so mad at myself for making such a stupid mistake" with "I am so grateful for the lesson I learned and how I have grown from it." This conscious shift in language creates ripples through your entire life experience.

Remember: Thoughts can be changed.

Here is one of many lovely passages from Louise's book:

"In the infinity of life where I am, all is perfect, whole, and complete. My life is ever new. Each moment of my life is new and fresh and vital. I use my affirmative thinking to create exactly what I want. This is a new day. I am a new me. I think differently. I speak differently. I act differently. Others treat me differently. My new world is a reflection of my new thinking. It is a joy and a delight to plant new seeds, for I know these seeds will become my new experiences. All is well in my world."

One particular exercise that I practiced in the beginning of my spiritual journey was taping up sticky notes all over my house with positive affirmations. When I was having a moment of doubt or fear, I would look at one of the notes, close my eyes, and gently say and feel the affirmation.

Here are some lovely affirmations that Louise used:

- *I love and approve of myself.*
- *I am enough just as I am.*
- *Every cell in my body is healthy and radiates health.*
- *I listen with love to my body's messages.*
- *I lovingly release the past. They are free and I am free.*
- *I deserve love, and I get it in abundance.*
- *I forgive myself and set myself free.*
- *I attract only healthy, loving relationships into my life.*

Affirmations alone won't change your life—but when combined with other healing practices, they can be highly effective. Their power lies in their ability to quiet the busy, distracted mind and redirect your focus toward more positive, empowering thoughts. Over time, this consistent redirection helps to rewire your brain, creating new, healthier patterns of thinking that support your growth and well-being.

So, the next step is to create a consistent meditation practice.

Meditation

"Prayer is asking; meditation is listening."
—Brownell Landrum

Meditation became central to my transformation. It is a way to hit the "pause button" each day. Meditation is not about stopping your thoughts, but rather a practice of learning to observe your thoughts without judgment. It's also about staying in the present moment – which I'll discuss more in the next chapter.

The word meditation means "to become more familiar with." When you meditate, you become more conscious and aware. Meditation can calm your nervous system, improves your mood, and allows you to cultivate inner peace and joy. It will raise your vibration and, thus, your ability to create and attract what you desire.

Meditation anchors you in the present moment. It cultivates awareness, stillness, connection, and allows us to experience life with greater clarity. It helps you experience life more fully, releasing attachment to thoughts and judgments.

I suggest a sitting practice. Start with five minutes or less, and gradually expand it. I always recommend using guided meditations to help you focus. The key is to be consistent. I can't stress this enough. You have to work your "meditation muscle" and develop it.

And let me nip this in the bud: When you say, "I can't meditate," the Universe is going to deliver that right back to you. What if you focused on the fact that "You can" meditate?

Every client that has come to me has been able to go into a deep meditation journey with me. Even on my TikTok live streams, I take people into a two-minute meditation with the Tibetan Singing Bowl, and they are shocked at how much better they feel afterward.

Many people experience what is called the "monkey mind." This is when you cannot stop the thoughts from rolling through your head and you are unable to sit still. Understand that, at first, you may do what I call "ping-ponging." You will focus on your breath, then your thoughts will wander, and then you'll return to your breath. Give yourself time to adapt to this practice.

If you cannot do a sitting meditation, there are other ways to meditate. For example, while you are out on a walk, focus on your breath, engage your senses, practice gratitude, and be present in the moment. tai chi, qigong, and yoga are also considered moving meditations.

Other forms of meditation include journaling, painting, drawing, singing, or playing music. Sound healing, grounding, and fire gazing are also great options. Choose what resonates with you, and be adventurous enough to try something outside your comfort zone. Pay attention to how you feel—the goal is to cultivate more inner peace and presence.

Research is increasingly showing that meditation and mindfulness practices impact how our genes express themselves. Meditation literally affects us at the DNA level. Epigenetics refers to how our genes express themselves. Dr. Bruce Lipton, a scientist who blends science with spirituality, has conducted research showing that 1% of disease is caused by genetics, while 99% is influenced by the environment and stress. Take a moment to think about this. For better mental and physical health, this is yet another great reason to begin your meditation practice!

A final word on meditation: some of you may be familiar with the story of Dr. Joe Dispenza. In 1986, at the age of 23, he was involved in a serious accident during a triathlon. While cycling, he was hit by an SUV, which resulted in six broken vertebrae in his spine. The doctors recommended a high-risk surgery, telling Joe that without it, he might never walk again.

Rather than opting for surgery, Joe chose to focus on inner healing techniques, using meditation and visualization to heal his spine. Nine and a half weeks later, Joe was able to walk again. He now conducts studies and speaks all over the world about how to rewire your brain for healing through meditation and visualization. His story truly demonstrates the incredible power of our minds!

The Power of Embracing the Present Moment

"Life is available only in the present moment."
— Thích Nhất Hạnh

There were so many moments in my life when the past haunted me and the future overwhelmed me. My mind would spin stories—of regret, fear, or what-ifs. But eventually, I learned that peace doesn't live in the past or the future. It lives in *this* moment. Right here. Right now. Healing, awakening, and clarity are only available when we're present.

Why Is It So Hard to Stay Present?

The mind is conditioned to drift. It's trained to analyze, compare, protect, fix. We're wired to scan for danger, replay painful moments, and anticipate worst-case scenarios.

But the truth is, the present moment is rarely as dangerous as our thoughts suggest. In fact, it's often full of calm, beauty, and possibility—if we're willing to pause and drop in.

During the most intense parts of my spiritual awakening, my mind became a battlefield. Fear. Doubt. Self-judgment. Whenever my mind started to race—spinning fears that weren't grounded in truth—I could feel anxiety slowly creeping in. Sometimes my thoughts pulled me backward into the past, where I would replay old choices and judge myself harshly.

The only thing that brought relief was presence. Meditation became my anchor.

When I returned to my breath, when I placed my hands on my heart and said, "Right now, I am safe," something in me softened.

My daily meditation practice has become essential in keeping me grounded in the present moment. Meditation always brings me home. It quiets the noise, settles the energy, and centers me again. In the stillness, I receive exactly the guidance I need—and I still do, every single day. Ideas flowed, and my nervous system settled. And I remembered: I am not my thoughts. I am the awareness behind them.

Presence isn't just about mindfulness—it's about remembering your *essence*. When we're present, we're more connected to our soul, our body, and our intuition.

We become better listeners. Better healers. Better creators.

Presence helps us:

- Feel our emotions without drowning in them
- Make aligned decisions.
- Truly connect with others
- Hear divine guidance.

A Practice to Come Back to the Moment

When you notice your mind spiraling, pause. Place one hand on your heart and one on your belly. Close your eyes and say:

"I'm here. I'm safe. I don't need to fix anything. I just need to breathe."

Take three slow breaths. Feel your feet on the ground. Listen for the sounds around you. Return to the rhythm of the moment. Staying present isn't about perfection—it's about remembering, over and over again, that this moment is sacred. Presence invites us to accept ourselves exactly as we are. Each time we come back to the present moment, it softens us into a place of gratitude, releasing judgement, even in the messy times.

How to Manifest Your Desires

※

"All you can possibly need or desire is already yours. Call your desires into being by imagining and feeling your wish fulfilled."
— Neville Goddard

Visualization is a powerful practice that uses mental imagery to shift energy and manifest your desires. I guide private clients through this visualization practice—leading them on inner journeys to connect with a memory of joy—it might be something in the present, near past, or even a childhood memory. When we debrief after the journey, clients are elated that they could connect so deeply with some joyful memories.

Some people have difficulty visualizing—that's okay. Even if visualization feels challenging, you can still tap into the emotional resonance—the *feeling*—which is just as powerful.

Visualization plays a key role in the manifestation process.

One of the great teachers of this work was Neville Goddard, a mystic and spiritual guide known for his teachings on imagination, consciousness, and creating reality. His most well-known principle was this: *you must embody the emotions of already having what you desire.*

When I read *The Neville Goddard Reader*, I was struck by his deep conviction that we each hold the power to shape our world through focused imagery and belief. Unlike many spiritual leaders of his time, Neville blended mystical insight with practical tools, always returning to this truth: consciousness is the creative force behind everything.

We can tap into this power through meditation—particularly in the theta state, where the subconscious mind is most receptive. The key is to define your desire clearly. Then, visualize a short, vivid scene that implies your wish has already come true. *Feel* the emotions—joy, peace, excitement—as if your manifestation is already real.

Another profound voice in this space is Abraham Hicks, a collective consciousness channeled by Esther Hicks. Abraham also teaches that *feeling* is the doorway to manifestation, aligning closely with Neville's message. Abraham speaks of the "Vortex"—a vibrational realm where everything you've ever desired already exists. She reminds us, *"Everything you want is in the Vortex, and the way to access it is by feeling good now."*

One final but crucial point: let go of the mindset of waiting. Waiting signals lack and creates resistance—it tells the Universe, "I don't have it yet." But when you release the idea of waiting, you close the gap between desire and manifestation. You align with the frequency of your desire—now.

Inspired Action

"Faith is taking the first step even when you don't see the whole staircase."
— Martin Luther King, Jr.

Aligned action is another key to manifesting.

Let me give you a recent example. I was guided by Spirit to look for a new car, which made sense given that I live in North Carolina, where the weather conditions vary. I had no clue how I would afford the $40,000 Subaru that I had my eye on, with $600 payments a month. I put that aside and went to work.

I spoke with two dealerships to get the best price. I then went to Carmax to get a quote on my current car, without mentioning that I would use it as a trade-in.

I wasn't concerned about the price. I was planting seeds. I began to visualize driving my new Subaru down the highway, windows and sunroof open, smiling ear to ear. I could feel the excitement in my entire body. I repeated this exercise daily to reinforce this belief. I had an inner knowing that it was already done.

The manifestation was effortless. After two weeks of practicing this visualization, I arrived at the dealership, we negotiated the trade, and I drove home a brand new 2025 Subaru Outback Limited Edition, far below MSRP, and with monthly payments that I could easily afford.

Let's do an exercise around visualization.

Close your eyes. I want you to imagine something you really want. It might be a romantic relationship, a job, a new home. Let this desire touch all of your senses. Picture every detail of what you desire. Feel that you have it right now. Feel the excitement and joy, smiling as you are thrilled that this desire has manifested.

Every home I've manifested has aligned perfectly with what I envisioned. I vividly imagine pulling up to the house, walking through the front door, exploring each room, and feeling the joy as if it's already mine. Each time, my vision has included a screened-in porch and a beautiful backyard—and each time, that's exactly what I've received for me and my cats.

Here's a second scenario: Visualize a time in your life when you achieved something you had truly longed for. It might have been a job, a relationship, a trip, or moving somewhere you had always dreamed of. Feel the excitement and joy you experienced. That's the exact emotional state you want to reconnect with whenever you're intentionally calling in something new.

Practice this daily and you will understand that you have an untapped power inside of you to co-create everything in your life.

Becoming a Death Doula

"Dying is nothing to fear. It can be the most wonderful experience of your life. It all depends on how you have lived."
—Dr. Elisabeth Kübler-Ross

After my job ended in 2018, my journey in Arizona came to a close, and I moved to a small town on the West Coast of Florida called Gulfport. After a year and a half living in an apartment there, it became clear that I needed my own space. I began the search for a home to purchase, despite warnings from others that finding an affordable home would be nearly impossible in that area. I stayed steadfast, setting intentions to find the perfect home—something open and inviting, with a lanai and a backyard for my cats.

Just as I was beginning to lose hope, a friend took me to a charming little village of mobile homes. As we drove through, we stumbled upon a house for sale. The owner invited us inside, and the moment I walked in, I knew it was perfect. It had a large lanai and a beautiful backyard for the cats and me. Within a month, everything was finalized, and I moved in.

Little did I realize that this move would allow me to tap into another ability and meet a new mentor. I would begin my journey as a death doula.

This mobile home park had an incredible location—just minutes from St.

The Magic Inside You

Pete Beach, Treasure Island, and Pass-A-Grille. The pool overlooked the Intracoastal Waterway, offering a serene spot to swim and watch sunsets. Having my own space was a breath of fresh air. I worked with a friend to install a permanent fence on one side of the yard, and the cats loved their new outdoor haven, complete with birds and squirrels to watch. The lanai became our favorite spot—a peaceful place to have my coffee and watch sunsets at the end of the day.

One of the most memorable residents was a kind man named Kenny, who came to the dock each evening to watch the sunset. His deep connection to nature—and the delight he found in watching pelicans dive and dolphins glide through the water—brought a smile to everyone who crossed his path. What I didn't realize was that moving to the park would lead to a powerful encounter with Kenny, one that would open a profound and unexpected chapter in my journey.

In May 2023, I learned that Kenny had fallen gravely ill and was diagnosed with a cancerous tumor in his back. One evening, I paddled by the dock in my kayak and stopped to chat with him and his daughter. It was clear he was weakening, but his spirit still shone brightly. Soon after, he became bedridden. On the night of May 26, 2023, I received a text from his daughter: "I understand you are a Reiki practitioner. I would like to book a session with you." She also expressed a desire for me to drum for her father at some point.

As soon as we hung up, I received a message from Spirit: "Go now."

I texted his daughter back and told her that I was being guided to drum for Kenny immediately. She got goosebumps and said, "Yes, I feel you are right. Please come over."

I prepared myself by meditating and praying, gathered my shamanic drum, and walked to their home. When I arrived, he lay in a hospital bed in their living room—frail and barely holding on. I placed one hand on his head and another on his heart, and then I began to drum. I entered a trance-like state, completely connected to Spirit.

At one point, tears streamed down my face. I later explained to the family that he was crying through me, mourning the life he was about to leave behind. He gave me a message to share: "Meet me on the dock."

I could see him in the tunnel, walking towards the light. He was a young man in this vision, and he asked, "Can I come back?"

I replied silently, "Your time here on this planet is complete. It's time for you to start your new journey."

I am not sure how long I drummed over his body, as I was in a deep, meditative state. Eventually, I was guided to stop. When I looked down at him, I noticed he was no longer breathing. On the last beat of my drum, he took his last breath. Gently, I informed the family that he had passed.

Feeling an undeniable pull, I immediately made my way to the dock Kenny had cherished so much. As I walked, dressed in white and carrying my drum, the HOA president stopped me to ask what I was doing. I shared that Kenny had just crossed over and that I was heading to the dock to pay tribute to him. Word spread quickly, and within minutes, more than ten residents gathered at the dock to honor him. He had chosen to transition during the sunset, a deeply poetic and beautiful moment.

This was my first experience facilitating a transition as a death doula, and it left me profoundly humbled. In all my years of readings and healings, nothing had touched me so deeply as helping someone cross into the light.

Following this experience, I reached out to a sixth-generation death doula named Paula in Gulfport. We met for coffee, and I shared my story with her. She explained that death doulas serve as channels and facilitators, guiding souls during their transition. Paula assured me that I didn't need certification or training. I already had the gift and would be called upon again.

She was right.

Soon after, I was asked to facilitate the transition of a woman in Arizona, who had not had food or water in seventeen days. The daughter was beside herself.

This would be my first virtual experience as a death doula. I prepared myself with a ritual of smudging, prayer, and intention, then astral projected to their home. Astral projection involves removing myself from my physical body, travelling on the astral plane (beyond physical reality), and literally feeling myself next to the person, regardless of distance.

As I drummed, I envisioned walking with her through a field of wildflowers on a mountainside. She shared a message for her daughter, and I felt her energy slowing, her heart rate easing. The next day, on April 11, 2023—a master number she had chosen—she passed peacefully.

Her daughter texted me, expressing immense gratitude for my assistance. I shared that I had found a heart-shaped piece of cat kibble during my preparations and sent her a photo. We both knew this was Spirit's way of affirming our connection.

In June of 2023, I was called on again. My friend Laurie called to let me know that her sister was in hospice. I shared that I was a death doula and that I could help her transition. She welcomed my support and said, "I don't want her to suffer. I would appreciate your help."

We coordinated a time that evening, when she and her sister's daughter would be present. Before the session, I prepared myself with meditation and prayer, then sent them a short video explaining the process.

During the journey, a herding dog appeared to guide her to the light. Laurie shared that it must have been her chihuahua. I told her, "No, a herding dog came through." This took Laurie's breath away. I learned that this was Kathy, a herding dog her sister had owned and loved deeply.

Early the next morning, her sister gently took her final breath, surrounded by her sister and daughter.

In September 2023, my mentor Paula reached out to me. She had a family struggling to let go of their ninety-one-year-old father, and she asked if we could perform the ceremony together. Paula sent me photos of him, and I began preparing for the session, which we scheduled for 8 p.m. on September 11th. Paula would be by the side of the family in Florida, while I would perform the ceremony at a distance in my home in North Carolina.

The following morning, at exactly 11:01, he gently transitioned.

After the ceremony, Paula shared that he danced in his chair—a clear indication of the "surge," a moment of energy often experienced before crossing over. While in the trance, Spirit showed me the numbers "111." I learned that these very numbers were tattooed on his arm.

She also shared an extraordinary detail about him—he was the engineer who invented an important part for the Apollo I spaceship. What an incredible honor it was to guide such a remarkable soul on his final journey, launching him into the light.

My next ceremony as a death doula was one I never expected: with my own family member.

My Aunt Marelyn was my mother's sister, and the two of them were incredibly close—they spoke on the phone every single day. Marelyn had a true gift for entertaining and was a marvelous cook. She worked in cosmetic stores that she and her husband created and owned. They were quite successful and were blessed to travel extensively all over the world.

Marelyn was a wonderful mother to my cousin Kim, and their relationship blossomed after Kim married and had three beautiful children of her own. They affectionately created my aunt's nickname "Gigi"—Gorgeous Grandmother. They shared some wonderful memories together as a family.

The last time I had seen Aunt Marelyn was at my mother's funeral five years prior. After my mom crossed over, I began to call Marelyn every day to fill the gap in my routine left by my mother. We became very close, and to my surprise, she deeply appreciated these short five minute phone calls. She always said, "Thank you so much for calling." My cousin Kim confirmed that these calls meant the world to her.

At one point, she became ill and was hospitalized, had a critical fall, breaking eight ribs. Her condition declined, and she was eventually brought home under hospice care. My cousin was aware of my work as a death doula, and one day she called me and asked me to do a virtual ceremony with the family.

I spoke to my death doula mentor Paula, as I needed her reassurance that I could proceed with a family member. She shared that death doulas often work with family members, as hers did. I took the day to prepare myself emotionally. My cousin, her three daughters, my twin brother, and one of the caretakers would be in attendance on FaceTime.

I opened with a brief meditation with the Tibetan singing bowl, focusing on gratitude for our journey with Marelyn. The next part involved playing my shamanic drum. This would help release her body from the planet. In trance, my Guides showed Marelyn walking through the most beautiful field, and she was amazed at the pure feeling of love. I could see her with my mother, and they were laughing together. I completed the ceremony briefly by playing my native flute.

Marelyn struggled to breathe after the ceremony. They scrambled to siphon liquid coming from her mouth. My mentor shared that she likely would have crossed over at this time, but it was clear the family was not quite ready, and there was still some unfinished business.

Having spent the better part of a month in the hospital, my Aunt had not had any time with her husband of almost seventy years. The day after the ceremony, my cousin finally had the strength to sit him down next to her to say goodbye. Over the next two days, it became clear he recognized and accepted that she was dying.

On Friday morning, January 25th, I was guided to offer Kim and her three girls a meditation. They accepted the invitation, and we all got on FaceTime. I took them into a lovely guided meditation, utilizing my calm voice and two Tibetan singing bowls. They all felt relaxed and more at peace afterward. I believe it also had an effect not only on them but on my aunt.

That evening, at 5:14 p.m., my Aunt Marelyn peacefully took her last breath. I found myself crying more for her passing than I did for my own mother. There would be no more phone calls—I would miss her beautiful presence dearly.

The day after she was cremated, my aunt came to me with a message for her daughter: "Make my chocolate bark for the Celebration of Life for everyone to enjoy." I called Kim to tell her, and she began the task of making my aunt's favorite dessert.

When I arrived in Massachusetts for the Celebration of Life, I told my cousin that I wanted the scarf I had crocheted for my aunt a few months earlier. Despite going through every closet in her condominium, I was not able to locate it.

The Sunday after the event, her family and I went out to lunch together. As I was sitting there, my aunt came through again. I wept as my aunt expressed her wish that they not carry heavy hearts, but instead move forward with joy in their lives. She showed me the Cirque du Soleil, and when I asked my cousin the reason, she shared that my aunt loved going to this show. This was simply the evidence she provided me with as proof it was her coming through.

When we returned to the condo, something magical had occurred. The caretaker shared that, for some unknown reason, she was led to the laundry room in the condo. She opened the cabinet, and there sat the scarf I had made for my aunt.

There is no denying that it was a coincidence. My aunt had come through to me with a message during lunch, and at that moment, the caretaker found the scarf.

With tears in my eyes, I placed her scarf around my neck—thank you, Universe.

Death As Transformation

"I've told my children that when I die, to release balloons in the sky to celebrate that I graduated. For me, death is a graduation."
- Elisabeth Kübler-Ross

You may have heard spiritual teachers refer to our planet as "Earth School." It's a place where we learn rich lessons in love, forgiveness, and courage. It's intense—and even brutal—at times. But this is not punishment. Our souls have chosen to incarnate here to grow in powerful ways. You are not here by accident. You chose to come, and Earth is your training ground for expansion. "Earth School" is one of the most rewarding places in the Universe because it is where we remember who we truly are.

When we incarnate, we experience "amnesia," forgetting our past lives. This forgetting is essential—it allows us to create new experiences, to learn, and to evolve. Amnesia gives us free will: the space to rediscover and remember ourselves through experience, rather than memory.

Every soul chooses certain life lessons before arriving—such as forgiveness, patience, self-worth, compassion, or unconditional love. The people we meet, including those who challenge us the most, are often part of soul agreements we made before birth. They are here to help us grow, even if it doesn't feel like it at the moment.

We choose our parents because they are often our greatest teachers. They're far from perfect and challenge us in countless ways. They may cause deep pain, yet they also trigger the wounds we are meant to heal—so that we can reclaim our power and live a meaningful, fruitful life.

We are spiritual beings having a human experience. And being human is not easy. Every heartbreak, every healing, every moment of awakening brings us one step closer to remembering our divine nature.

Our remembering is a return to love.

Some of you may have questions about life after death. As a medium—someone who communicates with those who have crossed over—I can tell you with certainty that our souls do transition to another place. I've helped clients connect with loved ones who've passed, and the messages they've received have brought immense peace. As an evidential medium, the loved ones always offer something personal and specific—an item, a memory, or a shared experience that only the client would recognize.

Once we've completed our time in this classroom, we return to the Spirit realm—not as the same person, but as an evolved version of our soul. We are transformed.

Many people fear dying so deeply that it's avoided entirely—even when someone is at death's door. This fear stems from not knowing what lies beyond. Families often resist giving their loved one "permission" to go. It's painful, and the heart doesn't want to let go. I witnessed this firsthand with my Aunt Marelyn. Her family wasn't quite ready to let her leave, but with support from me and my mentor, they gained a deeper understanding of death and its beauty. Marelyn was able to pass peacefully once they reached acceptance.

Death is a sacred transformation. It's not only our physical bodies that die—we also experience countless cycles of death and rebirth throughout our lives. Old parts of us must die to make room for the truest version of ourselves to emerge. It's much like the butterfly's metamorphosis.

Embrace death from a new perspective: you are returning home.

As a death doula, I've had the honor of walking people to the light. I can tell you—this passage is deeply beautiful. Those who have had near-death experiences (NDEs) often describe a profound sense of unconditional love—so powerful, so pure, they don't want to return to Earth.

I encourage you to read *Dying to Be Me* by Anita Moorjani. It's a profound memoir chronicling her extraordinary near-death experience and spiritual awakening. In 2006, Moorjani was hospitalized with end-stage lymphoma, her body ravaged by cancer. Doctors believed she had only hours to live.

What followed was a transformative experience that completely reshaped her understanding of life, healing, and identity. Her story goes beyond a typical illness memoir—it offers a spiritual perspective on healing. She reminds us that true healing comes from releasing fear, embracing self-acceptance, and understanding our deeper spiritual nature.

My Greatest Teachers

> *"When we are no longer able to change a situation, we are challenged to change ourselves."*
> — *Viktor E. Frankl*

Are you noticing a pattern in my journey? How things magically showed up in my life?

My relationship of ten years completely dissolved, my career ended, and I was left with one thing: to trust that the Universe was coordinating a better future for me. All of my spiritual work came to me as I surrendered.

In this chapter, I'll open up about the people in my life who caused me pain and trauma—and how, in many ways, they became my greatest teachers.

I have deep gratitude for all of them. I would not be the woman I am today, helping people all over the world who have experienced similar situations.

Here's a bit of my story. I don't live in this story anymore, but I share it so you understand that my journey, like yours, is not all rainbows and unicorns.

My mom, God love her, was a narcissist, and she married my dad unaware of his struggle with mental illness. Despite their challenges, she loved him deeply until the day he left the planet. We lived in a wealthy town in Massachusetts and I had access to the best of everything.

However, my mom did not know how to nurture me with love. Instead, she tried to fill the gap with material things. She was highly critical of me, and as a result, I never felt like I was enough. This led to deep issues with self-worth.

I struggled with a lot of digestive issues, which I believe were due to the tension in our home. Despite multiple tests with a specialist, no clear cause could be found. I tried to be the "fixer" of the family, cleaning the house for hours in an attempt to get my mother's approval. While I received praise for my efforts, it didn't seem to make a real difference.

My mom had me dieting at a very early age, despite not having a weight problem. As a result, my weight dropped, and so did my self-esteem. Her words were critical and harsh, and I internalized them deeply. My moods became increasingly low and were noticeable. Whenever the family was preparing for an event, she would say, "Are you going to ruin it for everyone?" Instead of nurturing me, and asking me why I might have been sad or upset, she would attack me, and selfishly ask me not to make everyone else miserable.

At eleven, I began running away from home. The pain in our household was suffocating. I would grab my orange knapsack and carefully pack my stuffed animal, Bronty, inside. The police would inevitably find me and return me home. By the age of sixteen, I had fallen into a very dark place. The constant arguing between my parents, my mother's gaslighting of my father, and the relentless bullying from my older brother had become unbearable.

One day, I walked into my mom's bathroom, opened the medicine cabinet, and took out a bottle of Valium. I poured the pills into my hand, staring at myself in the mirror, tears streaming down my face. I still remember my long hair pulled into pigtails and the overwhelming pain I felt in that moment. To this day, I don't know what stopped me from taking them—except, perhaps, an intervention from Spirit.

At the age of twenty-one, I understood the significance of my path in a career as a behaviorist. I never quite understood why I was led to work with differently-abled people, such as autistic and mentally challenged folks.

I discovered a picture in my mother's closet of my grandmother standing with a small red-headed girl with Down syndrome. I took my twin brother downstairs to the laundry room and showed him the photograph. He shared that he had been told that our sister had died.

Apparently, not.

My twin, Jed, and I have been incredibly close all our lives. We survived together. From a young age, we both found solace in nature—it was the only place that made us feel safe, protected, and grounded. When the chaos inside our home became too much, we would retreat outside. Jed, in fact, spent most of his childhood barefoot, connected to the earth in the purest way. Nature became our sanctuary, our escape, our shared language.

So when the long-buried secret of our sister came to light, it didn't completely surprise us. On some level, we had always sensed that there was more to our family story—something hidden beneath the surface, waiting to be revealed.

When it was confirmed that she was our sister, my trust with my mother was shattered. She called a family meeting and revealed that she had surrendered our sister, Stephanie, to the State and that she was still in contact with her. I was introduced to Stephanie shortly after, and I began to bring her home for the holidays.

Stephanie was a bundle of joy and quickly learned to recognize me, calling my name out in pure delight whenever she saw me. I am so grateful that I was able to integrate her briefly into our family before leaving home.

Finding out about Stephanie felt surreal. I couldn't comprehend how my mother had kept such a profound secret from our family for so many years. But what I learned next softened my heart and opened the door to compassion.

I discovered that Stephanie had been placed in a group home—and that my mom and aunt had been visiting her for years. Quietly, without telling anyone, our mother brought her clothes and took her out for her favorite spaghetti meal at Papa Johns. It revealed a side of my mother I had never seen—a quiet, nurturing love that had been hidden beneath the surface all along.

The situation then spiraled further when my mother learned of my sexuality as a lesbian. It shattered her dreams of watching her Jewish daughter walk down the aisle in a traditional wedding.

In an attempt to "fix" me, my mother sent me to Massachusetts General Hospital for a psychiatric evaluation, followed by regular therapy sessions. She thought "conversion" therapy would be the answer. The psychiatrists medicated me and I felt groggy, numb, and lifeless.

This challenge was further magnified by my father's mental health issues in our home.

My dad was a good-hearted man. He was diagnosed with paranoid personality disorder and was prescribed medications that caused noticeable side effects. At one point, he decided to stop taking them altogether. Despite his illness, my father was brilliant, earning two degrees in architecture and engineering from MIT in Boston. He was also an inventor, creating a three dimensional form to manufacture shoes, and even establishing his own company called Formulast. He also established the American Privacy Foundation and was committed to ensuring privacy for people globally.

My dad's mental illness worsened after he stopped taking his medication. The damage was irreversible, and the side effects—particularly the onset of tardive dyskinesia, which caused uncontrollable facial grimaces—were impossible to ignore. My mom, overwhelmed and unwell in her own way, sometimes responded with cruelty. She would mock his expressions, gaslighting him in a way that still stings to remember. Their marriage was unraveling, punctuated by constant arguments. I'll never forget one fight that ended with her shattering the glass kitchen table.

His obsession with privacy unfortunately impacted our lives. He installed a tally counter on the downstairs door to track how many people came in and out. I remember him dragging me to his car one day, insisting that it was bugged.

It was not easy living in our household, not by any means. My twin used to run out of the house when he heard my father's car pull into the driveway. Yet my twin and I survived, and we both realize it made us stronger in the end.

My mother and father did the best they could. They showed up in some meaningful ways, attending my swim meets and choir concerts. Mom always prepared wonderful meals for us, and Dad was always by my side, assisting with my schoolwork.

In many ways, they have helped me write this book—because everything they gave, and everything they couldn't give, prepared me to walk this path and offer what I've learned to others. For that, I am forever grateful.

The Forgiveness Journey with Mom

"True forgiveness is when you can say, "Thank you for that experience."
— Oprah Winfrey

How did I grow from this experience in a dysfunctional family? I learned to forgive. Here, you will witness my journey with my mother. Likely, you will shed some tears—I still do.

At the age of seventy-two, Mom underwent a difficult back surgery. She became addicted to opioids, suffered a critical fall, and needed to be permanently admitted to a nursing home. Much of her time was spent in a wheelchair. This became a pivotal time of healing for both of us.

Her time in the nursing home coincided with my spiritual awakening. Guided by my mentor, I came to understand the profound importance of forgiveness. It was time to release the resentment and anger I had carried for so long and let go of the pain that tethered me to the past.

At the time, I was living in Arizona, and I flew to Boston every four months, staying for five days to take care of her needs. I did this for over ten years. During my visits, one of the highlights of our time together was taking her to the local mall to shop for new clothes and necessities.

She adored going into different stores, and Macy's was our favorite, as they usually had the style and sizing she was accustomed to wearing. I sifted through racks of blouses and pants, holding them up for her approval.

Once we returned to her room, I'd remove all the tags and hang everything neatly in her closet. She always expressed her gratitude with a heartfelt, "Thank you, doll."

Each time I purchased new clothing, I would sort through all her belongings, discarding the worn-out items. Mom got a kick out of this and would giggle every time I tossed another piece of clothing on the floor to be thrown away.

Though I wasn't much for primping myself, I knew how important it was for her to look her best. I'd apply lipstick and rouge, then help her pick out earrings and other jewelry for the day. I even did her nails. She always smiled and said, "You did a wonderful job!"

As her independence began to fade, she slowly started to let me in. The walls around her heart began to melt—just like the Grinch! Her heart grew three sizes... and so did mine.

Helping her in ways she could no longer help herself filled my heart with joy. Spending twelve hours a day with her at the nursing home wasn't a burden—it was an act of love. A privilege, really. In those quiet, simple moments, we found a deeper connection than we ever had before.

The campus at her facility had expansive grounds with beautiful landscaping. On the days we stayed on campus, we took long walks— mom in her wheelchair, me pushing behind her. I fondly remember sitting in front of the building when it began to rain. I said, "Momma, let's catch raindrops in our mouths." And so, with joyful hearts, we did.

At one point, my partner and I brought my mother to Arizona to visit the National Parks. She was still using a walker and needed assistance, so we rented a van to make the journey more comfortable. Because she was incontinent, we lined the bed with protective blankets from the nursing home to keep her at ease throughout the trip.

We traveled to the Grand Canyon, Bryce Canyon, and Zion National Park. She absolutely loved gazing out the window, taking in the breathtaking landscapes as we drove. Her joy and childlike wonder made the experience unforgettable.

I will always be deeply grateful to Laurie—my partner of ten years and best friend for over twenty years—for making that trip possible. Though we parted ways under difficult circumstances in 2013, the separation ultimately became a powerful catalyst for my spiritual journey. And despite our ending, her relationship with my mother became one of the most meaningful gifts of my life.

That road trip became one of my mother's most cherished memories in her later years. By the end, we were all exhausted—but every moment was worth it, just to see her so happy.

One memory that truly stands out to me—and my twin—exemplifies the healing that occurred during this time. We were spending time with Mom in her room at the nursing home when, suddenly, she became upset and harsh with her words. Her anger caught me off guard, and I couldn't hold back the tears. Overwhelmed, I excused myself from the room.

A couple of days later, Mom and I were sitting in the café at her facility. Out of the blue, she turned to me with a thoughtful look in her eyes and said, "I made you cry the other day, didn't I?"

I replied, "Yes, Momma. What you said hurt me."

She paused, resting her hand under her chin, and said softly, "I am so sorry for making you cry." At that moment, a wall came down between us. For the first time, we were vulnerable with one another.

What made that moment so extraordinary was how out of character it was for her. My mother was not someone who apologized easily—if ever. Vulnerability was not something I often witnessed in her. Most of my life, she had been guarded, proud, and often critical. Emotions like regret or softness were rarely expressed, especially when it came to acknowledging the pain she had caused.

Her apology touched me deeply—it was a crack in the armor she had worn for so long, and through it, I saw a glimpse of the love that had always been there, hidden beneath the surface.

Mom then suffered two strokes, which left her unable to feed herself. She now entered a new chapter of her life, one that required me to care for her in a way I never imagined. Mealtimes became more than just routine; they became deeply nurturing moments. With care and patience, I fed her spoonful by spoonful, loving her in a way that deepened our bond. We would laugh together when the milk from her cereal dribbled down her face, turning what could have been an embarrassing moment, into one filled with warmth and laughter.

One day, my older brother called to tell me that Mom had slipped into a coma. I flew back immediately, knowing the time had come.

The family gathered, and I played my flute and drummed softly for her. One night, after my brothers and I went out for dinner, I returned alone to be with her. I heard odd noises as she breathed, and the nurse explained that this was called a "death rattle." The spots on her legs were another sign that she would soon pass.

Then, to my amazement, she opened her eyes and looked directly at me. I took both of my hands and cradled her face, saying, "Momma, I love you. It's time to go to God."

I was exhausted and decided to leave at 9:30 p.m. that night. A few hours later, she transitioned to begin her new journey. It was October 26, 2019—a date that marked a new chapter in my life.

Exactly two weeks later, Mom found a way to reach us all. My older brother sent me a text: *"I heard the song 'Dust in the Wind' today and thought of Mom."* Hours later, my twin brother called. He and our older brother hadn't spoken in years, yet he shared the exact same experience—the same song, the same thought of Mom. Neither knew about the other's message.

I immediately understood the sign. Back in 2008, *"Dust in the Wind"* was the first song I learned on guitar. I used to play and sing it in the nursing home while Mom and the other residents listened. She was sending us a clear message—she was at peace, watching over us still.

I cherish these experiences with my mother, as they showed me the power of unconditional love and forgiveness. She will forever be in my heart.

Tony Robbins: Unleash the Power Within

"The cure for the pain is in the pain."
— Rumi

I had been writing this book on and off for almost two years, and I reached a point where I simply couldn't continue. Something inside me was blocked.

A dear friend of mine, Kevin, reached out and said, "Spirit says we have to attend the Tony Robbins event in November."

I replied, "What? I'm not even a fan of his." But Kevin was clear—Spirit said we *had* to go. Trusting my intuition, I immediately said yes.

I couldn't ignore Kevin's invitation because of several synchronicities. In 2018, when I opened my practice, my brother told me he believed my path would be similar to Tony's—he's a huge fan of his.

Then, at a spiritual gathering, an astrologer read my chart and said my energy aligned with Tony's. Even more surprising, I had unknowingly been doing dance parties at the end of each of my live streams on TikTok—something I later learned is a core part of Tony's events.

As the date approached, I entered the experience with no expectations. My only real concern was the size of the crowd—15,000 people. How would I react? What would I learn? And how would I grow? I knew Tony had been doing this work for almost forty years, but I wasn't sure how his methods would affect me personally.

The day arrived—November 14, 2024. I flew into Newark, New Jersey, checked in, and got a good night's sleep at my Airbnb. The next morning, I arrived at the venue, buzzing with energy. As I stood in line, I chatted with attendees who had been to many of Tony's events. Their enthusiasm was contagious.

The music began to blare, Tony came on stage, and the entire room leapt to its feet, dancing and jumping. The energy was electric—I felt it in every cell of my body. Over the next four days, we dove into his teachings, working through a detailed workbook and absorbing insight from a lineup of handpicked speakers. Each day lasted twelve to fifteen hours. Despite the little sleep and sparse meals, I felt more energized than ever before.

One of the methods that Tony used during the four day event impacted me greatly. It was another catalyst that shook me to the core to finally believe in myself. We experienced a process known as the Dickens Pattern–named after Charles Dickens, inspired by *"A Christmas Carol,"* where Ebenezer Scrooge is visited by the Ghosts of Christmas Past, Present, and Future — this led to dramatic transformation.

The Dickens Process is designed to help you break through limiting beliefs by experiencing the emotional pain they've caused in the past, the cost they're causing in the present, and the devastation they'll cause in the future — *if you don't change them now.*

I cried as we did this exercise, just like many others in the audience.

I felt the weight of what it would cost me to keep living under the same false beliefs.

At that moment, I knew — I couldn't carry them any longer.

I realized that the real reason I wasn't writing this book was because I believed it would have no value. Deep down, I didn't believe my healing journey could help anyone else.

But the pain of that belief was too much to bear. Something shifted. And in that shift, I began to see the truth: My story does matter. My voice has value. And what I've walked through might just light the way for someone else.

I also came to realize that I had been carrying something called *imposter syndrome*. It's that quiet, persistent doubt—the belief that our successes are somehow accidental, that we're not truly "qualified," and that we don't deserve the recognition or rewards we've received.

Releasing that belief changed everything. It had a profound impact on my private practice. For the first time, I felt confident about raising my prices—because I finally understood the true value of what I was offering. And the results were undeniable. People continued to book sessions with me, confident in the value that I would provide.

When I returned home, I was invited to join the Tony Robbins Facebook community. I posted a few reflections and soon received a comment that would shift the course of who would edit and publish my book. I connected with Tom, an audiobook producer, and we spoke on the phone. This simple exchange eventually led me to my editor in the UK. Once again, the Universe was dropping breadcrumbs to align the right team of people to help me with my book.

After just one Zoom call with Catherine, the editor in the UK, I knew she was the right person to do the developmental editing for my book. For the next month, I wrote every single day, and the words flowed effortlessly. I realized during this time that I would need a publisher, so I asked the Universe to send me the right one.

I met with several publishing companies, but none felt quite right. Tom agreed—their prices were far too high for what I needed. So I kept searching. Eventually, an acquaintance introduced me to a friend who might be able to help. On our Zoom call, Aelah and I felt an instant energetic connection. She was a fellow energy worker, Princeton-educated, and currently taking courses in publishing. She had already published her own work. The final confirmation came when I found out she lived in Traveler's Rest, South Carolina—remember my connection to that town from my previous trip?

During our conversation, I asked if I could share an insight from Spirit. She agreed. I told her she was meant to open a publishing business. To my surprise, she admitted she'd been considering it. Aelah's business, Mother

Tree Publishing, took on my project. At last, I knew I was on the right path—and fully prepared to publish my book properly.

The Importance of a Role Model

> *"Role models set the pattern for our lives. They show us who we can become."*
> — Unknown

During Tony's event, one speaker's journey stood out among the rest: Jamie Kern Lima. Her story of resilience and determination was truly inspiring. Earlier in the book, I discussed the importance of finding a role model.

Why is this important? Because purpose can feel lonely at first.

When we begin to awaken to our deeper calling, there's often no clear path in front of us—just a restlessness that says, "There is something more for you." A role model becomes a living example that it's possible. They remind you that the road may be unfamiliar, but it's not unwalked.

A role model reflects your potential back to you. They help dissolve the doubts, the imposter syndrome, the fear of being "too much" or "not enough." You see in them a version of yourself—maybe a few steps ahead—bravely doing what you long to do.

They normalize the extraordinary. They anchor your vision in real-life possibility. And most importantly, they inspire *action*. As you step into your deeper purpose, a role model becomes not someone to copy, but someone who gives you permission to be more *you*.

So, when Jamie appeared on stage, her presence immediately touched my soul, and I knew I could walk her path in my own special way. Here is Jamie's story…

Jamie began her career as a local television newscaster, battling a skin condition called rosacea and hyperpigmentation. Her professional turning point came during a broadcast when her makeup failed to conceal her skin's blotches. Rather than succumb to embarrassment, she saw an opportunity: creating her own cosmetic line.

Working tirelessly with dermatologists and scientists, Jamie founded IT Cosmetics. The path was far from smooth. For three years, doors remained closed. Undeterred, she worked grueling hundred-hour weeks without paying herself. When an investor cruelly suggested she was too overweight to sell cosmetics, she used his negativity as fuel.

Her breakthrough came through QVC, where she was given a high-stakes ten-minute window to sell her products. Defying conventional advice, Jamie showcased her cosmetics using models with real skin conditions. The gamble paid off—she sold out her entire inventory in less than ten minutes, launching her into unprecedented success.

In 2016, L'Oreal acquired IT Cosmetics for $1.2 billion, and they appointed Jamie as the first female CEO of the company. Forbes soon recognized her as one of America's Richest Self-Made Women.

Jamie's most profound lesson resonated deeply with me: trust in your inner knowing. Her unwavering belief that her vision would come true resonated with me. She believed in her heart and soul that she would be successful.

Everything that is meant for you will not pass you by. You must have unshakable faith and trust in the Universe's plan. You must remain intentional and stay open to the broader plan. Follow your heart and your yellow brick road.

One Size Does Not Fit All

> *"We are not all meant to walk the same path, and that is the beauty of life."*
> — Anita Moorjani, *author of* Dying to Be Me

The methods I've shared worked for me. However, there is no "one size fits all." While many of these tools are foundational for anyone seeking growth and change, every journey is unique. Take what resonates and allow yourself to create your own path.

As you begin this journey, remember: healing isn't linear. There will be highs and lows, moments of clarity, and times of doubt. But every step forward—no matter how small—brings you closer to the life you're meant to live.

Use your spiritual toolkit as a source of strength and resilience. Use it daily, adapt it as needed, and trust that you are exactly where you need to be. Choosing to grow and heal is a powerful act of self-love, and you are worthy of every beautiful transformation that follows.

Change is never easy. Healing takes time, patience, and a deep commitment to unraveling old, conditioned patterns. This process creates space for new thought patterns—ones that align with the life you truly desire.

It's important to remain curious and open. Growth isn't about finding one perfect solution or teacher—it's about exploring, experimenting, and discovering what truly resonates with you.

Stay open to learning. Seek out teachers and mentors who challenge and inspire you. Try different techniques, practices, and modalities to shift your energy and expand your awareness.

I can't stress this enough: finding the right mentors and teachers is essential to your journey. If you truly want to transform your life, you must be willing to invest in yourself. Every dollar I've spent on my personal growth has returned to me in infinite ways—in wisdom, healing, and deep inner peace. This isn't just an expense—it's the foundation for everything you are becoming.

So, are you ready to begin?

Your new life awaits.

The Journey Back to Love

> *"Love is the great miracle cure. Loving ourselves works miracles in our lives."*
> — Louise Hay

The core of our healing is falling in love with ourselves. It's an interesting notion, isn't it? We're so accustomed to falling in love with someone else.

But what if you could fall in love with *you*?

This is a profound remembering—a return to who we truly were when we first entered this world. I believe that healing the past is a journey back to love. When we learn to love ourselves unconditionally, releasing all judgment, we create space for the abundance, joy, and connection we were always meant to receive.

You incarnated in this life to grow through many lessons. Loving yourself means actively choosing joy. It means reclaiming your power and setting healthy boundaries. Too often, we allow others to diminish us because we've internalized the belief that we are unworthy of love or respect. But that belief is a lie. You are inherently deserving of love, kindness, and genuine respect—simply because you exist.

Self-love is a holistic practice—an integration of mind, body, and spirit.

Nourish yourself fully. Prepare wholesome meals. Meditate. Move your body. Explore mindfulness practices that light up your soul. Every action becomes a love letter to yourself.

As you establish daily rituals to care for your energy, they will become what I call "non-negotiable" habits. Nothing will interfere. The excuses will fade. And you'll come to understand that choosing *you* is the deepest act of love you can offer yourself.

Over time, your words, thoughts, and actions will begin to align with a deeper appreciation for who you are. Perfection is not the goal. Embrace your flaws and imperfections. They're not mistakes—they're the beautiful details of your unique story.

Now imagine the magic of loving yourself completely—exactly as you are, with all your radiant imperfections. You don't need anyone's approval but your own. In this vibration of pure, unconditional love, you become your own source of power. Your own source of light.

And that magic? It's already within you.

When you become the essence of love, you elevate your vibration—and that's when you invite the real magic into your life.

Unbecoming: Final Thoughts

"Maybe the journey isn't so much about becoming anything. Maybe it's about unbecoming everything that isn't really you."
— Paulo Coelho

Life is no longer what it used to be when I was in a relationship or working in the traditional world. As I watched everything unfold, I realized that I was simply not the same person. As a gifted channel for healing, a psychic, mentor, death doula, inspirational speaker, and now author, I know my purpose is to touch lives.

I had always longed to know and embody inner peace. But the thing about peace is, we can't chase it. We must allow ourselves to embody it. It's about mastering your essence.

My childhood home was my unexpected teacher. Growing up in a dysfunctional family, I never experienced a true sense of "home." Even as I bought homes throughout my life, I never felt settled or embraced the responsibility of owning them. I resisted this–just as I resisted making a peaceful home within myself.

Forgiveness is the alchemy that transforms pain. When we release fear, judgment, hate, jealousy, anger, and resentment—we return to love. As simple—or perhaps as complex—as that may sound, I believe love is the ultimate solution.

But from this place of inner peace, I realize there is no more resistance. Unbecoming the person I had been—by healing past traumas and learning to love myself—allowed me to flow through life with ease and grace. I no longer need anyone's approval. The opinions of others hold no weight. I am no longer codependent. I have now become sovereign.

There is no shortcut to spiritual growth. To "unbecome" yourself, there are no easy answers. Time, patience, and surrender are essential parts of the process.

What I've come to realize is that the most powerful changes on the spiritual path are often the most subtle. It's not always some huge breakthrough or life-altering moment. Sometimes, it's simply noticing that when my mind starts spinning fears—stories that once consumed me—I don't fall for them anymore. I don't get pulled under. Or when I drift into the past, replaying old choices with regret, there's a softer voice now... one that gently says, *"It's okay. You're safe now."*

That's the journey. Not always dramatic, but deeply transformative.

Everything is temporary, and life can change in a moment's notice. Stay present—this is where you create your future.

We tend to beat ourselves up, believing we should be further along or "doing better." But the truth is, we're shedding the parts of ourselves that no longer serve us. Expect a push-pull as you go through this process. You may want to control the outcome, but what we often fail to see is that the Universe has something far greater in store. This is where patience comes in.

The discomfort of unbecoming is real—and at times, overwhelming. But I can assure you: the struggle and the wait are worth it. The unraveling of old conditioning, paired with the release of the past, will guide you toward a version of yourself that is more authentic, empowered, and free.

Your superpower is love.

Remember: the magic is already inside of you. It's time to tap into it...

Afterword

Dear Reader,

First, I want to thank you from the bottom of my heart for purchasing my book. It means the world to me.

I would be absolutely delighted to hear from you. If my story has touched you, inspired you, or awakened something magical within, please feel free to email me at lisabromfieldenergyhealer@gmail.com. Your words would bring so much joy to my heart.

My intention with this book is to take the message even further—to speak live to audiences all over the world. At these events, I'll be sharing more intimate details of my journey. I would love the chance to meet you in person, to give you a big hug, and, if you'd like, personally sign your copy of the book.

If you know of a venue or event where my story could be shared, I would be honored if you reached out.

I hope this book has inspired you to explore some—or all—of the ideas and tools shared within its pages.

Trust your inner guidance.

Let your heart lead you to the healing practices that resonate most deeply.

Seek out your teachers—the energies and messages that feel aligned with your heart and soul.

I also invite you to visit my website, where you'll find a variety of resources and offerings. Most of my healing services are available virtually, allowing

Afterword

us to connect no matter where you are located.
May your journey lead you to the love you have always deserved.
And always remember: *the magic is inside you.*

Thank you again for your love and support.
　With all my heart,
　Lisa Bromfield

Sources and Inspirations

This book is the result of many years of integration, healing, and inquiry, supported by the wisdom of many teachers, mentors, and researchers. The following works, among others, deeply influenced the ideas shared in these pages:

- **Anita Moorjani's** memoir *Dying to Be Me: My Journey from Cancer, to Near Death, to True Healing* (Hay House, 2012)
- *The Artist's Way: A Spiritual Path to Higher Creativity* by **Julia Cameron** (TarcherPerigee, 1992)
- *The Four Agreements* by **Don Miguel Ruiz** (Amber-Allen Publishing, 1997)
- *You Can Heal Your Life* by **Louise Hay** (Hay House, 1984)
- *A Course in Miracles* by **Helen Schucman** (Foundation for Inner Peace, 1976)
- *The Vortex* by **Esther and Jerry Hicks** (Hay House, 2009)
- **Dr. Rick Hanson**, *"The mind is like Velcro for bad experiences and Teflon for good ones"*—You can find this insight and more in his book *Hardwiring Happiness: The Practical Science of Reshaping Your Brain—and Your Life* (Harmony Books, 2013), as well as on his website: https://rickhanson.com/velcro-for-the-bad-teflon-for-the-good/
- A study from **Johns Hopkins University School of Medicine**, led by

Dr. Roland Griffiths, explores the profound and lasting impact of psilocybin on depression. The article titled *"Psilocybin Relieves Depression for Up to a Year"* (2022) is available at: https://hub.jhu.edu/2022/02/16/psilocybin-relieves-depression-for-up-to-a-year/
- **The Earthing Movie**, available on YouTube and at the official website: https://earthingmovie.com
- **Dr. Bruce Lipton**, a pioneering biologist who blends science with spirituality, can be found through this article published by the *National Library of Medicine:* **https://www.ncbi.nlm.nih.gov/pmc/articles/PMC5367557/**

To all these authors, researchers, and storytellers—thank you.

Praise for Lisa Bromfield

"Lisa is a Blessing to our world. The time I spent with her (virtually) was second to none. Her gifts truly changed the trajectory of my life. The insight I gained from my session with Lisa empowered me to release things I had been holding on to that were not good for me and open my mind/heart to endless possibilities. She empowered me to begin unapologetically walking in my truth! Her authenticity and unique positive energy are what initially caught my attention. Her endearing spirit and wisdom are what have kept me present. So, whether it's guidance, healing, reiki or one of the many other things Lisa offers, I assure you that you will be more than pleased!! If you have found her, it's for a reason."
  - Cathryn Konrad

"Lisa is an incredible and radiant soul whose energy is truly unmatched. I feel so blessed to have experienced a distant Reiki session with her. Although I've had in-person Reiki sessions before, none have been as powerful as my time with Lisa—she is the real deal. During our session, we focused on forgiveness, and as a result, something truly life changing happened. My father, who has struggled with addiction since his teenage years, has finally chosen to check into rehab at 53. This breakthrough is nothing short of miraculous, and I know Lisa's healing energy played a role in making it possible. Lisa, thank you for sharing your light, guiding me on this journey, and helping me find peace. I am forever grateful for your presence in my life."
  - Rosalinda Sanchez

Praise for Lisa Bromfield

"Lisa is a true healer. She performed a healing session with me and it was spot on. She knew exactly what I needed to hear. My grandma who died during childhood unexpectedly came through and it was such an added bonus that made my heart so full. I didn't know exactly how much I needed this session until it was over. I got the best sleep I've had in years. She gave me multiple resources and contacts for my interests and gave me so much insight. She told me how to cleanse and protect myself and my space. She is such a blessing."
-Katy Miller

"Lisa is an amazing psychic and delivers messages from a place in the heart. Lisa recently did Death Doula work to facilitate and assist in helping my sister Linda cross over. Linda was in hospice with cancer. I didn't want her to suffer. I had heard about Lisa's work and contacted her for her help. We set up a time in the evening; Linda's daughter and I sat by my sister's side. Lisa did this work remotely, as we were in Georgia and she was in North Carolina. Lisa explained what she would be doing in the ceremony, releasing my sister's body through the use of her shamanic drum. When she was finished, she texted us. My sister passed away the next morning. Lisa shared messages that came through during the ceremony. A cattle dog came through to guide Linda to the Light, and Lisa had no knowledge of the fact that my sister had owned a Shetland Sheepdog many years ago, named Kathy. When my sister passed away the next morning it was so comforting to know that Kathy was there to walk her on her new journey. I can't thank Lisa enough, and I highly recommend her to anyone who needs a Psychic and/or Death Doula."
-Laurie Campbell

Made in the USA
Coppell, TX
13 June 2025

50699884R00095